Pearson
PUBLISHING

ICT Explained
A teacher's guide to ICT terminology

DERRY
KEY SKILLS
RESOURCE
CENTRE

Gareth Williams

Illustrations by Matthew Foster-Smith

Further copies of this publication may be obtained from:

Pearson Publishing
Chesterton Mill, French's Road, Cambridge CB4 3NP
Tel 01223 350555 Fax 01223 356484

Email info@pearson.co.uk
Web site www.pearsonpublishing.co.uk

ISBN: 1 85749 765 1

Published by Pearson Publishing 1999
© Pearson Publishing 1999

Second edition 2001
First reprint 2002
Second reprint 2003

Contents

Introduction

Information and Communication Technology in general and computers, in particular, have profound implications for education. As a consequence, it is vital that teachers become familiar with the required vocabulary and terminology and develop their understanding of how the various technologies affect their professional life.

ICT Explained provides a convenient source of reference and support. It is presented via four main parts as follows:

- Part 1 Anatomy of a computer
- Part 2 Computer operation
- Part 3 Software
- Part 4 Data protection and health and safety

An index at the back will help you to find specific information.

It has been written to form a coherent whole if read through but can equally well be dipped into as required. This book concentrates on computers, their peripherals and uses; little reference is made to more familiar ICT tools such as telephones, television and video recorders.

This, the second edition, has been written to cover the basic concepts in Information Technology as required by the ECDL (European Computer Driving Licence).

If you have any comments or suggestions as to how this book may be improved, please send them to the author via Pearson Publishing.

Structure of a computer

IT (Information Technology) and the more recently-introduced term, ICT (Information and Communication Technology), is the use of modern digital electronic technology to process and communicate information. The development of powerful low-cost computers is at the forefront of this technology. The diagram below shows a simple structure for the operation of a computer:

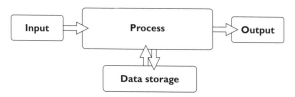

Input

The need to capture data quickly and accurately has led to a wide range of input devices being developed. These devices make use of human touch, light, magnetism, sound and control sensors. Each type of input device has been designed for a specific purpose.

Process

In microcomputers, the main processing chip handles the instructions from the computer program and processes the data. Most home, school and business computers use only one processor or CPU (central processing unit, see page 6), but larger systems like network servers may have two or more processors.

Data storage

Computers need both long-term and short-term storage. Long-term storage, for example, saving a graph to be printed, is performed with a hard disk. Floppy disks, CD-ROMs and magnetic tape are also examples of long-term storage devices. Short-term storage, for example, remembering subtotals in a calculation, is more closely linked to the processor and uses RAM memory (see page 6).

Output

The results of processing are passed to output devices. The most common output devices are the computer monitor and the printer.

Anatomy of a PC

The following pages describe a typical computer system known as a PC (personal computer) which is found in homes, schools and businesses. It is a type of microcomputer.

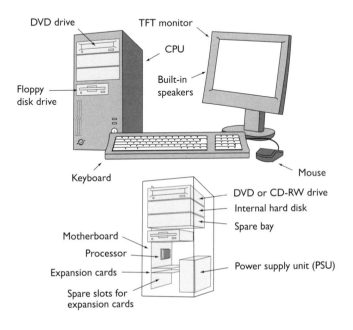

A modern desktop PC with cut-away showing internal features

A PC is a small desktop microcomputer, typically built around a single printed circuit board called a motherboard. The PC consists of three basic parts: a base unit (containing the processor, memory and disk drives), a keyboard (and mouse), and a monitor. Additional devices (known as peripherals) can be connected to increase its functionality.

Modern technology has allowed portable equivalents of desktop computers to be made. These portable (notebook) computers combine the basic parts into a single unit. Although notebooks have the advantage over desktop microcomputers in size, weight and portability, they are usually not as powerful, they are more expensive and will not allow standard interface cards to be slotted in.

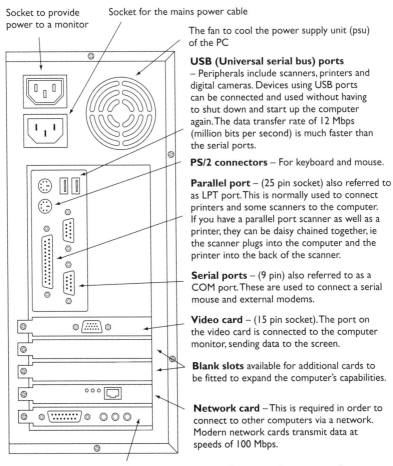

Socket to provide power to a monitor

Socket for the mains power cable

The fan to cool the power supply unit (psu) of the PC

USB (Universal serial bus) ports
– Peripherals include scanners, printers and digital cameras. Devices using USB ports can be connected and used without having to shut down and start up the computer again. The data transfer rate of 12 Mbps (million bits per second) is much faster than the serial ports.

PS/2 connectors – For keyboard and mouse.

Parallel port – (25 pin socket) also referred to as LPT port. This is normally used to connect printers and some scanners to the computer. If you have a parallel port scanner as well as a printer, they can be daisy chained together, ie the scanner plugs into the computer and the printer into the back of the scanner.

Serial ports – (9 pin) also referred to as a COM port. These are used to connect a serial mouse and external modems.

Video card – (15 pin socket). The port on the video card is connected to the computer monitor, sending data to the screen.

Blank slots available for additional cards to be fitted to expand the computer's capabilities.

Network card – This is required in order to connect to other computers via a network. Modern network cards transmit data at speeds of 100 Mbps.

Sound card – This card provides the connections for a microphone input and speaker output.

Note: A port is the name given to the connection/interface between a PC and a peripheral.

The connectors at the rear of a modern desktop PC

Hardware and software

There are two parts to a computer system, the hardware and the software. The term hardware is used for any of the physical parts of the computer, eg the monitor, keyboard, etc. The software refers to the computer programs, eg the word processing software or the operating system. Both are equally important for a functioning system.

Input devices

This chapter describes some of the input devices you might see in use with a typical PC. Other less common ones are described on pages 19 to 32.

Keyboard

The most common way of entering data into a computer is through the keyboard. The layout of the letters on the keyboard is standard across many countries in the world and is called a QWERTY keyboard. These are the first few characters on the top row of letters.

A QWERTY keyboard

Mouse

The movement of the mouse by the user's hand is mirrored by the pointer on the monitor screen. Under the mouse is a ball which rolls as the mouse is moved. This movement of the ball causes two shafts to rotate inside the mouse, one shaft records the movement in the north–south direction and the other shaft records the east–west movement. When the screen pointer is over an icon or menu selection, the mouse button can be clicked, double-clicked or dragged (moved with the button held down) to activate a process.

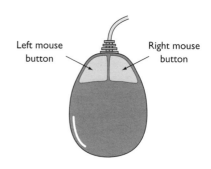

Left mouse button

Right mouse button

Some mice have a small wheel as well as the buttons. The function of the wheel depends on the software being used on the computer: in a document, it can allow the user to scroll up and down; in a desktop publishing package, it might enable the user to zoom in and out of the page. Over a period of time, the performance of the mouse can deteriorate as the ball and shafts collect dust and dirt. Many modern mice use a light beam and detector to register movements instead of the mouse ball. Some mice now use infra-red or wireless links to the computer which removes the need to have a connecting cable.

Scanners

Scanners enable both pictures and text to be input to a computer. Scanning text in order to recognise the words and letters requires special software and this is covered under optical character recognition on page 29.

The most common type of scanner is the flat-bed, but smaller and cheaper hand-held scanners that are rolled over the document/picture are also available.

The flat-bed scanner works by placing the picture to be scanned face down on a glass plate like a photocopier. A bright light is slowly moved across the picture and the reflected light is focused onto a bank of light sensors using mirrors and lenses. White reflects the most light and black reflects the least. For each tiny part of the picture, the strength of the reflection is captured and converted into a digital signal for input to the computer.

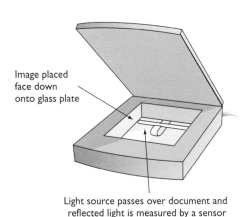

Image placed face down onto glass plate

Light source passes over document and reflected light is measured by a sensor

A flat-bed scanner

Scanned pictures, which can be manipulated using sophisticated image editing software, are often used in publishing work.

Process

Processor (CPU)

The processor is the part of the computer which does much of the hard work. It takes information from the input devices, and instructions and data from memory, processes the information as required, and then sends the result to storage, or to an output device.

Processors inside modern PCs include the Intel Pentium III and 4, Intel Celeron and AMD Athlon.

The speed of the processor is one of the factors that determine the performance of a computer. The speed is measured in megahertz (1 Mhz = 1 million cycles per second) or gigahertz (1 Ghz = 1000 million cycles per second) and a typical value for a Pentium 4 would be 1.5 Ghz. Other factors that affect performance include the amount of RAM memory (see below) and the hard disk size (see page 8) and speed at which data can be accessed from the disk (see page 11).

Types of memory

All computers have memory to store instructions and data. There are two main types of memory:

- RAM (random access memory)
- ROM (read only memory).

Random access memory

The RAM is a temporary storage for data. The typical amount of RAM in a home computer might be 128 MB (see page 7). As the computer is started, operating instructions, computer programs and data are moved into this memory as required. The RAM clears when the computer is switched off, which is why it is important to save your work to disk when you finish.

Read only memory

ROM is memory stored in a chip which is not lost when the power is turned off. On most computers (eg PCs), this memory is quite small but it contains the essential instructions to enable the computer to check the hardware and load operating systems from the disk in order to start.

How data is stored in computer memory

Bits

Computers are constructed of electronic circuits. Through these circuits there can be two states – electricity can be flowing or not flowing. When a pulse of electricity is present we call this a '1' and the absence of electricity is a '0'. The transistors on the silicon chips can store a 'bit' (**binary digit**) which is either the 0 or the 1.

Bytes

A byte is a unit of memory in the computer. It is made up of eight bits, in other words a byte can store eight 0s or 1s. Each character from the keyboard is given a code consisting of eight bits. These codes are the same internationally and are called the ASCII code (American Standard Code for Information Interchange). The code for the letter 'a' is 97 or 01100001. Each character therefore is held in one byte of memory. One byte is a very small amount of storage and it is more usual to refer to kilobytes (KB), megabytes (MB) and gigabytes (GB).

- 1 kilobyte = 1024 bytes (2^{10})
- 1 megabyte = 1024 kilobytes = 1 048 576 bytes (2^{20})
  – approximately 1 million bytes
- 1 gigabyte = 1024 megabytes = 1 073 741 824 bytes (2^{30})
  – approximately 1 thousand million bytes
- 1 terabyte = 1024 gigabytes = 1 099 511 627 776 bytes (2^{40})
  – approximately 1 million million bytes.

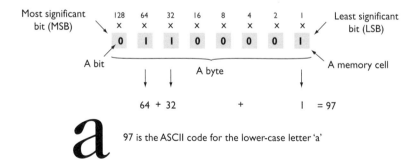

How the letter 'a' is stored in computer memory

Data storage

A storage device retains its contents when the computer is switched off and is used to hold programs and data. All computers have some form of hard storage.

Hard disks

Hard disks are a common form of data storage in most computers, both on stand-alone and networked computers. A typical microcomputer purchased for home or school would have a disk capacity of 20 gigabytes. This would hold the operating system (eg Microsoft® Windows), applications (word processor, spreadsheet, database, etc), games and the data from programs. On larger systems, the hard disks may hold terabytes (1024 GB) of storage.

Data is stored by magnetising the surface of a flat, circular plate. These plates rotate at high speed, typically 60 to 120 revolutions per second. A read/write head floats on a cushion of air a fraction of a millimetre above the surface of the disk. It is so close that even a smoke particle on the disk would cause the heads to crash. For this reason, the drive is inside a sealed unit.

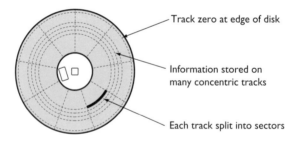

Tracks and sectors on a hard disk

Programs and data are held on the disk in blocks formed by tracks and sectors. Moving directly to data on a disk drive is called random access.

Floppy disks

Floppy disk drives can be found on most microcomputers and accept 3.5 inch floppy disks. High density floppy disks for a PC hold 1.44 MB of data. Floppy disks are useful for transferring data between computers and for keeping a back-up of work files. Back-up disks should be kept safely away from the main computer for security reasons.

Floppy disks only spin when loading or when saving needs to take place. Floppy disks rotate more slowly than hard disks, at only six revolutions per second.

Compact discs

CD-ROMs are 12 cm diameter plastic discs which can hold large quantities of data (650 MB) in the form of text, sound, still pictures and video clips.

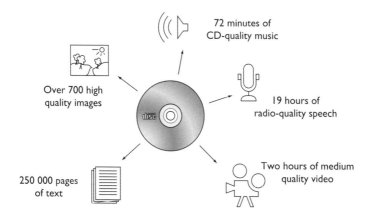

72 minutes of CD-quality music

Over 700 high quality images

19 hours of radio-quality speech

250 000 pages of text

Two hours of medium quality video

The data is stored on the surface of the disc as minute indentations and is read by a laser light. CDs are available in three forms:

- **CD-ROMs** – The letters ROM in the name mean read only memory. In other words, you can only read from the disc, not write or store data onto it. This type is the most common sort of CD available and is the way most software programs are sold. It is a memory storage device but would not be considered as a 'backing store' as the user cannot write to the disc.

- **CD–R** – These CDs are initially blank but, using a special read/write CD drive unit, the user can store programs and data onto the disc. These discs can only be written to once.

- **CD–RW** – These are similar to the 'R' type but the user can read, write and delete files from the disc many times, just like a hard disk.

Both CD-ROMs and CD-Rs can be referred to as WORM devices. This stands for **w**rite **o**nce **r**ead **m**any times. A standard CD unit will only allow discs to be read and the data/programs stored onto your computer's hard drive. To write data to CD-R and CD-RW discs, a 'writeable' CD drive unit must be used – these are more expensive than ordinary CD drives.

One of the most important areas of use is in education and home entertainment where a wide range of discs are now available. Text and graphics from some CD-ROMs can be copied into the word processing software on the computer and then edited and printed. (Note: Care should be taken to ensure that copyright is not breached.)

DVDs

DVDs (the term originating from digital versatile disc or digital video disc) are now replacing CD drives in computers. DVD units are likely to replace home CD systems and VHS tapes. The success of DVD is largely due to the huge memory capacity of the disk and the high quality of stored images. DVDs can store up to 17 GB of data, the equivalent of 26 CD-ROMS (or the capacity of nearly 12 000 floppy disks). This equates to eight hours of full-motion images together with sound tracks and subtitles.

Watching a film stored on DVD format has significant advantages over VHS video tape. The digital images and sound tracks produced from the DVD are of a higher quality and the user can move to any part of the film immediately. In addition, the high quality digital images and sound do not deteriorate with constant use as they do with the magnetic VHS tapes. Films sold on DVD often include extra features such as different language sound tracks and subtitles, commentary from the director, interviews with the cast and explanations as to how the special effects were created.

Magnetic tape

Magnetic tape can also be used as a backing store for permanent storage. Data is saved along the tape in blocks, separated by 'interblock gaps'. Just like the tape in a tape-recorder, the data is written to or read from the tape as it passes the magnetic heads. One disadvantage of tape storage is that you cannot go directly to an item of data on the tape as you can with a disk. It is necessary to start at the beginning of the tape and search for the data as the tape goes past the heads – this is called serial access.

As magnetic tape is relatively cheap, tapes are often used to take a copy of hard disks for back-up (security) reasons. One popular magnetic tape unit, similar in size to a computer hard disk unit, is called a tape streamer. These units use tape cassettes that can store very large quantities of data, typically tens of gigabytes. The cassettes can then be kept in a safe place away from the computer.

Removable media

There are other common devices, such as zip and jaz drives, which are similar to floppy drives, in that individual disks are removable and portable, yet they hold much larger amounts of data (typically between 100 MB and 2 GB).

Disk access times

For a drive to read data from a disk, the read/write head must move in or out to align with the correct track (this is called the seek time). Then it must wait until the correct sector approaches the head. The time it takes to do both these things is called the disk access time. It sounds very short (about 15 milliseconds for a typical hard drive), but can be very significant when accessing or searching through large amounts of data (eg in a large database). Floppy disks and CD-ROMs have longer access times than hard disks. The following table offers a comparison of different data storage devices:

Device name	Approximate cost	Capacity	Direct/serial access	Access speed
Hard disk	£100 unit	20 GB	Direct	Very fast
Zip disk	£180 unit £20 disk	250 MB	Direct	Fast
Magnetic tape	£600 unit £20 tape	26 GB	Serial	Slow
Writeable CD-ROM	£150 unit £2 per disc	650 MB	Direct	Medium
Floppy disk	£30 unit 50p disk	1.44 MB	Direct	Medium

File sizes

Files from different software packages, even though they contain similar information, can take up quite different amounts of disk space when stored. For example, the word 'Hello' is five characters long and, as each character is held in one byte of storage, it occupies five bytes of memory. The following table shows the size of the file when the word 'Hello' is typed into the following packages and then saved to disk:

Software package	File size	Description
Notepad	1 KB	The word is saved just as text (.txt) with no formatting. Although the word is only five bytes long, in the Windows operating system there is a minimum file size typically 1 KB (1024 bytes).
Microsoft® Word (Office 2000)	19 KB	The text has been saved together with a considerable amount of formatting data associated with the word processor package (.doc).
Microsoft® Word (Office 2000) In Rich Text Format	2 KB	The details associated with Word have been removed but the file still holds formatting information, eg font size, style, bold, italic, etc (.rtf).
Microsoft® Paint	2305 KB	The word 'Hello' has been typed into the Paint package (.bmp). The file is saved as a bitmap image and includes details of the text and all the background information.

Files that can hold particularly large quantities of data and therefore require considerable disk storage capacity are database files. It is possible to estimate the approximate storage requirements by calculating the storage for a single record and then multiplying this by the potential number of records in the database file or table. In the simple example on the right, a single database table containing four fields is considered. (More information on database tables is given on pages 87 to 96.)

Field name	Type	Length
Title	Text	35
Author	Text	30
Publisher	Text	30
ISBN	Text	15

Books database table

One record, or the details of one book, will occupy approximately 110 bytes of data (35 + 30 + 30 + 15). If the table held details of four million books then the file size would be approximately 440 MB. This is only approximate as other hidden characters may be saved with the data (eg 'end of field' and 'end of record' markers) and one megabyte is actually 2^{20} bytes = 1 048 576 bytes (see page 7).

Output devices

This chapter details some of the output devices you might use with a typical PC. Other less common ones are described on pages 19 to 32.

Monitor

The computer monitor, screen or VDU (visual display unit) is the most common output device. Screen sizes are still quoted in inches and popular sizes are 15 inches (38 cm) and 17 inches (43 cm). The size is always measured diagonally, from corner to corner, but beware, the size of the screen you see may be less than the quoted size as some of the glass is hidden behind the plastic rim of the monitor casing. The screen sizes for televisions are also measured in the same way. Larger monitors make working at a computer easier on the eyes and are essential for use in desktop publishing and design work.

Most monitors utilise cathode ray tubes (CRTs) to display the image. However, portable computers and the more modern flat-panel displays utilise liquid crystal displays (LCDs), thin film transistors (TFTs) or field emission displays (FEDs) (see page 14), with other possible methods currently being researched.

Flat-panel displays are popular as they take up far less room and seem likely to replace the traditional CRT monitors. They are, however, more expensive, although prices are falling.

The spacing of the pixels (short for picture elements) on a monitor determines the clarity, or resolution, of the screen image. Three standards in current use are:

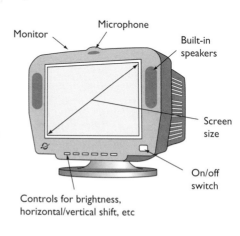

- VGA (Video Graphics Array) 640 x 480 pixels

- SVGA (Super Video Graphics Array) 800 x 600 pixels

- XGA (Extended Graphics Array) 1024 x 768 pixels

A conventional CRT monitor

Cathode ray tubes

Conventional monitors are similar in many ways to the television. They use cathode ray tubes containing an electron gun at the back of the tube which fires electrons at phosphor dots coating the inside of the screen. When struck by the electrons, the phosphor dots glow to give the colours. Because you sit very close to a computer screen and need to be able to read small text, these dots need to be very close together. On a colour monitor, a set of dots is made up of a group of three colours: one green, one blue and one red dot. One group of three dots is called a pixel and a typical distance between the pixels on a computer monitor is 0.28 mm.

Liquid crystal displays

Liquid crystal displays utilise tiny crystals which, when a charge is applied across them, polarise the light passing through them. Used in combination with special filters, this means that light will not pass through when an electrical charge is applied. LCDs are also used in watches and calculators.

TFT screen

A more advanced type of display, giving a full colour and high quality output, is the TFT (thin film transistor) active matrix screen. Each pixel on the screen is controlled by its own transistor, this provides a higher resolution and more contrast.

Field emission displays

Field emission display screens use two thin sheets of glass a millimetre apart, separated by a vacuum. The back glass is made up of millions of tiny tips that can be switched on and off and fire electrons at the front screen across the vacuum. When the phosphor dots are hit by the electrons, they glow to produce bright, sharp images.

Printers

Over the years, many types of printers have been made with different print mechanisms. These printers can be placed in one of two groups – impact printers and non-impact printers. With impact printers the letters, or tiny pins which make up characters, strike an inked ribbon against the paper. Because of this hammering effect these printers can be quite noisy. Today, the most popular types of printer for schools, offices and homes are ink-jet and laser printers, which are non-impact printers.

Dot-matrix printer

A dot-matrix printer has a printhead that travels across the paper. In the head are a set of pins which shoot out and strike the ink ribbon against the paper as the printhead moves along. These printers produce low to medium quality black and white printing. Several years ago they were the ideal choice for a home printer but now the colour ink-jet has taken their place.

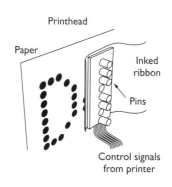

Ink-jet printer

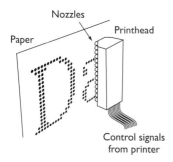

In an ink-jet printer, the printhead contains tiny nozzles through which ink can be selectively sprayed onto the paper to form the characters or the graphic images. Inside the printhead are tiny piezoelectric crystals. These crystals change shape when an electric current is applied across them and this forces the ink out through the printhead nozzle.

The bubble-jet printer is a type of ink-jet printer but instead of the ink being forced out of the printhead, it is heated rapidly. This causes the ink to boil and a bubble of ink is formed. As the bubble forms, it expands and is forced through the nozzle of the printhead and onto the paper.

These printers are very quiet and can produce relatively high quality black and white or colour printing.

Laser printer

Laser printers work on the same principle as photocopiers. The toner, which is powdered ink, is transferred to the paper where it is fused by the action of heat and pressure. Lasers are very quiet printers and give high quality print. A school or business printer would have a typical speed of 12 to 24 pages per minute (ppm). The majority of laser printers sold are black and white, but colour laser printers are becoming increasingly popular as their prices fall below £1000.

Types of computer

For many years, computers have been placed into different groups according to their size, performance and cost. With the rapid development in computer technology, a new group has appeared, the personal digital assistants (PDAs), and the traditional minicomputer group is largely disappearing as microcomputers and computer networks become more powerful. The different groups are described below:

- supercomputers
- mainframe computers
- minicomputers
- microcomputers
- PDAs
- embedded computers.

Supercomputers

Supercomputers are the fastest and the most expensive computers. They have huge processing power and are used mainly for scientific and engineering applications. This power makes them suitable for applications such as weather forecasting and complex graphical techniques. A supercomputer recently built by IBM (International Business Machines) is able to perform ten trillion mathematical calculations per second using 8200 processors working in parallel. Computers of this size and power can cost £100 m.

Mainframe computers

Mainframes are used in large companies for data processing and by scientists for complex mathematical calculations. They can have hundreds of simultaneous users. Mainframes have also found a new role as network servers on the Internet. On average, a mainframe would cost £4 m. An example of a mainframe is IBM's System/390.

Minicomputers

Minicomputers may be used by smaller businesses to manage their data processing needs. Complex programs like relational databases run efficiently on these computers and older database programs can be linked to newer programs running on the Internet.

The cost of a minicomputer is around £30 000 and an example is IBM's AS/400 or iSeries. The role of minicomputers is being replaced by microcomputers and computer networks as these become more powerful.

Microcomputers

Desktop computers

The computers we use at home, in school and in most businesses are called microcomputers. There are many different makes and models to choose from when buying a microcomputer but ones with a CD-ROM or DVD drive, stereo sound, a modem and software are available for around £1000. The type and speed of the processor broadly determine the power of the computer. A typical processor is the Intel Pentium 4 running at 1.4 Ghz (1400 million cycles per second). Since microcomputers were first introduced, the speed of processors has increased year by year. Several manufacturers are now shipping 64 bit processors running at 2 Ghz (1 gigahertz = 1000 megahertz). Although this trend is likely to continue, there has recently been a new demand on manufacturers to develop processors for portable devices like Internet mobile phones. These processors need to be smaller and use much less power in order to conserve the batteries in these portable devices.

Notebooks

Modern notebook computers are light and easy to carry around. They are approximately 30 cm across, 20 cm back and 3 cm deep and can weigh less than 1 kg. The screen is on the inside of the top flap that hinges open. Notebooks have many of the features that are available on desktop computers including CD/DVD drives, floppy disk drives, modems and the sockets at the back to connect to printers and monitors. The keyboards have the same layout as desktop computers although the keys are more compact and notebooks use touch pads or a button to control the screen pointer. For ultra-light and thin notebooks, the DVD and floppy drives can be placed in a docking station that also contains the battery charging unit and connections for the printer. The user will then slip the notebook into the docking station when they return home or go into the office. Although notebook computers have the advantage over desktop microcomputers in size, weight and portability, they are usually not as powerful, are more expensive and will not allow standard expansion cards to be slotted in.

Personal digital assistants (PDAs)

These are small hand-held computers generally only 12 cm long by 8 cm wide and less than 2 cm deep. These personal electronic organisers have software for keeping a diary, holding contact details, making notes, sending and receiving emails and playing games.

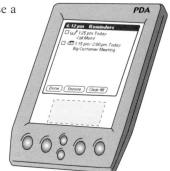

Because they are so small, most PDAs use a touch-sensitive screen and a stylus (pen) rather than a keyboard to input data. Software is then used to recognise either the user's handwriting or accept letters selected by the stylus from a screen display of the keyboard. Docking stations are often used with PDAs so that batteries can be recharged and data, for example, diary entries, can be updated with desktop PCs.

Embedded computers

From telephones to missiles, and from cameras to washing machines, many modern devices contain built-in computers or embedded systems. There is no need for these systems to use keyboards and computer monitors since the inputs required come from the device's sensors, and outputs control the operation of the device.

Intelligent and dumb terminals

On a school network, the workstations are microcomputers that can run programs and process data. The programs, for example a spreadsheet, are downloaded from the server and are run under the processing power of the workstation. These are called intelligent terminals. Where organisations and businesses run minicomputers, mainframe or supercomputers, the workstations effectively only need to be keyboards and screens. As data is entered at the terminal, it is passed to the central computer where the processing takes place. The results of the processing are then passed back to the user's screen. These are called dumb terminals, as they have no facilities to process data at the terminal. With the continuing decrease in the cost of computer-processing power, dumb terminals have become less common, but are beginning to be fashionable again under the name 'thin clients'.

Other peripherals

The need to process data quickly and accurately has led to the development of many types of input and output device. The majority of the devices mentioned in this chapter can be used in different school situations. Each type of input or output device has been designed for a specific purpose.

Where input and output devices might be used in school

The following examples illustrate where some of the input and output devices/techniques mentioned in this chapter might be observed in schools:

- **Actuators** – include motors which might be found in the flat-bed plotter in the Design and Technology department; hydraulics such as in a school lift; pneumatics in a robot arm; and solenoids to control the flow of gas in the heating system.

- **Bar code reader** – used on student ID cards for automatic registering or parcels arriving to the main school office by companies like Parcel Force.

- **Concept keyboard** – often used with younger children to input data by pressing on pictures, drawings and words.

- **Control devices** – include light-dependent resistors which are used to measure the hours of sunshine on the school weather station; switches for controlling the school bells or heating system; and thermistors for measuring temperature in a school Science experiment.

- **Digital camera** – all departments for capturing digital pictures, eg taking pictures of activities for the school Web site.

- **Display systems** – include liquid crystal display panels and projectors found in many classrooms.

- **Graphics tablet** – used by the Art and Design department to trace and draw using the stylus.

- **Interactive whiteboard** – in an ICT suite or subject classroom for teaching and training.

- **Light-emitting diodes** – used in Design and Technology for making working model traffic lights, etc.

- **Magnetic ink character recognition** – seen on cheques in the finance department.

- **Magnetic stripes** – used on identity cards for registering students.
- **Musical Instrument Digital Interface** – used by staff and students in the Music department for composing and editing.
- **Optical character recognition** – for capturing text-based material for teaching notes and administration.
- **Optical mark reader** – used for entering the students' answers from multiple-choice test papers directly into the computer.
- **Plotter** – used in Design and Technology for drawing accurate plans.
- **Smart card** – used in the mobile phones of staff and students.
- **Sound and speech** – used by staff with weaker typing skills to enter student information into computerised reports. Spoken output may be used with blind students.
- **Touch screen** – used in the main entrance foyer of the school, together with a general information program, to guide and help visitors.
- **Video digitiser** – used by many departments when creating presentations using multimedia software.

Actuators

Signals from computers can generate physical movement in certain control devices. These devices are called actuators and include:

- motors
- pneumatics
- hydraulics
- solenoids.

Motors

The output of a computer can be used to drive small stepper motors. With stepper motors, each electrical pulse from the computer rotates the motor shaft by a tiny amount. For a typical motor this might be a turn of $1.8°$ which would mean 200 pulses would be needed to turn the shaft of the motor through one complete revolution.

Stepper motors give very precise movements and can be used on devices such as flat-bed plotters or a robotic arm.

A stepper motor

Hydraulics

Here the output from the computer controls the movement of hydraulic rams by pumping oil. These hydraulic rams, similar to those seen on mechanical diggers and bulldozers, can be slow but are very powerful.

Pneumatics

Pneumatics are quite similar to hydraulics in using rams but the pistons are powered by air rather than oil. Pneumatics are not as powerful as the hydraulic systems but the movement of the system is very fast.

A robot arm can be controlled by motors, hydraulics or pneumatics. The type of system used depends on the application, ie:

- most accurate movement – motors
- fastest movement – pneumatics
- most powerful – hydraulics.

A robot arm

Solenoids

Solenoids are coils of wire where, when electricity flows through them, the coil becomes an electromagnet and draws the shaft into the centre of the coil inward. Computers can output signals to operate the devices.

The movement of the solenoid can be used in many ways, eg to open latches and locks or to control the flow of gases and liquids in pipes.

Bar code reader

Bar codes are made up of black and white stripes of different thicknesses. These lines represent numbers and are read with a wand or laser scanner. They are now used on almost all goods sold in shops and supermarkets, and provide a fast and reliable method of entering data even when the surfaces being read are curved.

The numbers of the bar code hold coded information about the product, including the country of manufacture, the name of the manufacturer, a product item code and a check digit. They do not hold information directly for the name, description or price of the product. When the numbers on the bar code are scanned, the data is passed to the computer which then returns information about the product.

Concept keyboard

A concept keyboard consists of a flat-bed of contact switches covered by a flexible membrane. Programmers can allocate one or more switches to respond in different ways. Overlays with pictures and symbols are placed over the membrane. Uses of the concept keyboard include primary schools where the overlays are designed with interesting picture layouts. Children press on particular symbols or pictures in response to the activity being done. These keyboards are very flexible: an overlay for a five-year-old can be designed quite differently to an overlay for a ten-year-old which would be more detailed.

Concept keyboards are also used in restaurants where the checkout tills use symbols to speed up the data entry. They can also be used in hostile environments, for example on North Sea oil platforms, where the keyboard allows workers to use computer-controlled machinery through the keyboard without it being damaged by the salt spray or chemicals on the platform.

Control devices

There are many different input devices associated with controlling machinery and monitoring and logging the environment. Three of the simplest and most common devices are switches, and light and heat sensors. There are also sensors for pressure, stress and strain in materials, air pressure, humidity, pH sensors to measure acidity, etc.

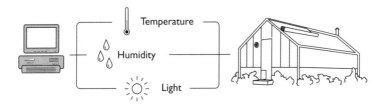

Greenhouse control

Light-dependent resistors (LDRs)

Light-dependent resistors are light sensors that change their electrical resistance according to the amount of light falling on them. The brighter the light, the lower the resistance. These, together with heat sensors, could be used in a computer automated greenhouse to maintain the ideal growing conditions for the plants.

Switches

When computer input comes from mechanical devices like automated machinery in factories, switches can be used. Mechanical switches such as slide, toggle and push buttons can be activated by an operator or moving equipment.

Magnetic switches are activated when a magnet comes close to the switch. The two contacts which form the switch come into contact in the magnetic field.

Thermistors

Thermistors are electronic devices that can be used to measure temperature since their resistance changes with temperature. Using this device, the computer can input the temperature and respond accordingly, perhaps by switching on or off other circuits controlling heaters.

Digital camera

The picture taken with a digital camera is stored in computer memory rather than on film as in an ordinary camera.

The different colours that make up the picture are converted to digital signals (codes of 0s and 1s) by sensors placed behind the lens. These pictures can then be displayed directly onto the computer monitor or imported into a graphics/art package for editing. The quality of the picture is determined by the resolution of the camera and is measured in pixels (see page 13). High-quality digital cameras may have a resolution of three or more megapixels.

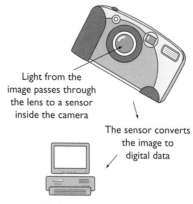

Light from the image passes through the lens to a sensor inside the camera

The sensor converts the image to digital data

The image can now be stored or loaded into a computer

Many cameras have their own small LCD (see page 14) screen which displays the picture taken with the camera. This gives the user the option to view the picture and discard it if it is not suitable. The cost of taking pictures with a digital camera is much less than an ordinary camera where a film and processing has to be purchased. An ink-jet printer (see page 15) and high-quality paper is all that is needed for printing digital pictures.

Display systems

There are three methods for enlarging the screen image for an audience to see. These are:

- increasing the size of the computer monitor (ie to become a display monitor)
- projecting the image onto a screen using an LCD panel and overhead projector
- projecting the image directly onto a screen with a projector.

In situations where everyone in the room would benefit from seeing one screen, the ability to project the screen image onto a large screen is particularly valuable. It might be that the teacher or trainer wishes to demonstrate the features of some new software. It might be the delivery of part of the lesson using a presentation package like Microsoft® PowerPoint or, in a business meeting, it might be the presentation of new products or sales figures. Display systems are becoming increasingly popular as prices fall and the technical specifications improve.

Display monitors

Display monitors generally vary in size between 26 and 42 inches and are particularly good for data that is constantly being updated, eg the arrivals and departures screens at railway stations. Display monitors have bright, steady displays that also make them suitable for software training and demonstrations. They are particularly heavy and bulky units so they are not suitable for portable use. They are also less flexible than the modern projection systems described on the next page.

LCD panels

The signal from the computer is passed to a liquid crystal display panel which is positioned on an overhead projector. Panels are the least expensive option in the range of display systems. Another advantage of the LCD panel is its portability; the unit is lightweight and fits into a small carrying case.

The projected image is not very bright, particularly on colour panels where the light has to pass through several layers of crystals. It is important to use a powerful overhead projector and best results are achieved in a darkened room.

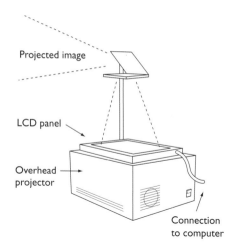

Projected image

LCD panel

Overhead projector

Connection to computer

Projectors

Units that connect directly to the PC and project a bright, sharp image on the screen are becoming increasingly popular in schools and business organisations. The light source for the projector is either a halogen lamp or, even brighter, a metal-halide lamp.

All projection systems have certain key features. These include:

- **Resolution** – Projection devices can project images in VGA, SVGA or XGA mode (see page 13).

- **Brightness** – The brightness of the projected image is very important and will determine the size of the screen used and the light levels in the room. Brightness is measured in lumens. 800 lumens might be the typical output of a projector.

- **Colour** – Most projectors can display 16.7 million colours.

- **Audio system** – Small speakers are often built into projectors but in larger rooms additional output may be required.

- **Mounting** – Projectors are generally set up on a table in front of the screen or on the ceiling.

- **Remote control** – These are generally infra-red devices. They have a laser pointer to point at the screen and to control the mouse and the functions on the projector.

- **Bulb life** – Bulbs for projectors can be very expensive. In the early systems, the life expectancy of a bulb was around 30 hours. In modern units, this has increased to 2000 hours.

Graphics tablet

The graphics tablet is a flat pad which the user can write on, or draw on, with a device similar to a pen called a stylus. The surface of the pad is sensitive to the position of the stylus and the stylus itself is sensitive to the pressure applied by the user. As the stylus is moved across the pad, the movement is translated to a drawing on the computer monitor. The harder the user presses on the stylus, the thicker the line drawn on the screen. A typical resolution for a graphics tablet used in art work and computer aided design (CAD) is $1/1000$ cm.

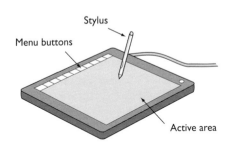

Stylus

Menu buttons

Active area

Interactive whiteboard

The interactive whiteboard is similar in appearance to a traditional whiteboard. The surface is designed for dry marker pens, but it is also ideal as a projection surface as it has a non-reflective matt finish. Behind the surface of the board is a grid of copper wire that detects the position of the pen and relays the co-ordinates back to the computer, either by a cable link or by a remote infra-red connection.

Image projected onto whiteboard so it can be viewed by all

User can annotate and interact with displayed image

The board is most effective when used as an input to a computer running a projection unit and software. This is described on page 25. In addition to using board marker pens, the teacher can use an electronic pen whose position can be determined by the grid without the need for the pen to contact with the surface. The pen acts in a similar way to a computer mouse; pressing the electronic pen on the board acts as the left mouse button. With software packages projected onto the board, the teacher can point and click using the electronic pen. Images can be drawn and manipulated, and the teacher can interact with other software, run CD multimedia sequences and access the Internet to enhance the lesson content and understanding.

Small, A5 and A6 size, graphic tablets are also available that link to the interactive whiteboards through an infra-red connection. This tablet allows the teacher or student to write onto the main board from anywhere in the classroom. The graphics tablets also allow teachers to prepare the lesson material beforehand, independent of the main whiteboard.

Joystick

Joysticks are popular input devices for computer games. The hand grip can be moved around the central axis in any direction but is spring-loaded to return to the centre when the hand pressure is released. Joysticks have many more buttons to control the software functions, for example, when using a joystick to control a flight simulator, the buttons control the flaps, views from the cockpit, landing gear and engine speed. Some joysticks have 'force feedback' which enables the user to feel some of the forces that might be experienced in real life.

Light-emitting diodes (LEDs)

1.8-20 mm

LEDs are small electronic components which emit light when a voltage is placed across them. They are low power devices which can be seen on the front of a computer to show when the disk drive operates or when there is network activity. They are also used to monitor the logic state (on and off) in control applications.

A light-emitting diode

Light pen

Light pens are not a very common input device but they are useful for design work and drawing on the screen. They do not, as the name suggests, emit light but a sensor at the end of the pen detects the light from the screen. The specialist light pen software can determine the position of the pen by timing how long it takes for the electron beam, scanning backwards and forwards across the monitor, to reach the pen. Some pens have a button on the tip so that they can simulate the actions of the mouse.

Magnetic ink character recognition (MICR)

This method of inputting data into a computer is used on bank cheques. The numbers printed at the bottom of a cheque have magnetic particles in the ink. These can be read very quickly by machines (as many as 3000 cheques per minute). Three numbers are printed on a cheque: the cheque number (each cheque in the cheque book has its own number); the bank or building society's sort code; and the customer's account number.

When a cheque is written and presented to the bank, a fourth number is added using the special magnetic ink which can be read by the computer. This last number to be typed on the cheque by the bank is the amount the cheque is made out for. MICR is very reliable as a means of entering data into a computer because it can still be read even if someone scribbles over the numbers with a pen.

Magnetic stripes

Magnetic stripes are thin strips of magnetic tape, often found on the back of plastic credit and debit cards. When the card is used, the stripe passes playback heads, similar to a tape recorder, which reads data from the stripe.

Cards with stripes are used, for example, to withdraw cash from cash dispenser machines (called automatic teller machines or ATMs) in the walls of banks, building societies and shopping centres.

In schools, cards like these can be used to control access, track pupil attendance and use of equipment such as photocopiers by departments or individual members of staff.

Musical instrument digital interface (MIDI)

MIDI was developed as a standard for linking musical keyboards together. Computers fitted with MIDI interface boards can be connected to MIDI instruments, allowing the music being played to be stored and displayed by the computer on the monitor. The computer can display the music as a musical score and notes can be added, altered or deleted. The music being played can also be printed out from the computer.

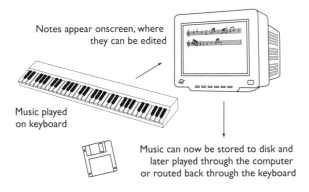

Notes appear onscreen, where they can be edited

Music played on keyboard

Music can now be stored to disk and later played through the computer or routed back through the keyboard

Optical character recognition (OCR)

Scanning devices are also used to recognise letters, numbers and words. The ability to scan the characters accurately depends on how clear the writing is. Scanners have improved to be able to read different styles and sizes of type and also neat handwriting.

One application of optical character recognition is reading postcodes on letters at sorting offices so that letters can be sorted automatically.

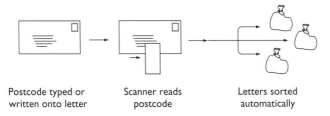

Postcode typed or written onto letter

Scanner reads postcode

Letters sorted automatically

Optical mark reader (OMR)

Optical mark readers detect marks made on paper. It is usually recommended that the marks are made with a soft (HB) pencil. The reader scans across the paper with an infra-red light. Where there is no mark, there is a strong reflection of light off the white paper; where a mark has been made, the reflection is reduced.

This form of input is often used for students' answers to multiple-choice examination papers and for choosing the numbers on lottery tickets.

Plotters

There are several types of plotter. The flat-bed plotter, commonly found in the Design and Technology departments of schools, uses precision motors controlled by the computer. These motors move an arm across the paper in the 'x' direction and the pen unit up and down the arm in the 'y' direction. An electromagnet lifts and drops the pen onto the paper.

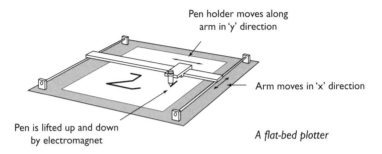

Pen holder moves along arm in 'y' direction

Arm moves in 'x' direction

Pen is lifted up and down by electromagnet

A flat-bed plotter

Plotters are often used in science and engineering applications for drawing building plans, printed circuit boards, machines and machine parts. They are accurate to hundredths of a millimetre and, although plotters found in schools may take A3 or A2 paper, flat-bed plotters can be the size of a small classroom. However, the increase in the quality of low-priced A2 and A3 size colour ink-jet printers has reduced the demand for the new, smaller plotters.

Smart cards

A smart card (also known as an integrated chip card, or ICC) is a plastic card that contains a tiny microprocessor chip. This enables more data to be stored on the card and also enables the personal identification number (PIN) entered by the user to be checked against the information held in the chip. Smart cards are more secure than cards with magnetic stripes but they have not been widely adopted by banks because of the cost of changing all the cash machines (ATMs). Smart cards are used more extensively in mobile phones and satellite television receivers.

Sound and speech

Most computers have the facility to play high-quality sound, from music programs, music CDs, CD-ROMs and DVDs. You can even buy music online, and download it either to your computer, or a special portable player, similar to a Walkman®, called an MP3 player. As well as having music played by the computer, it is also possible to have spoken output. This is particularly useful for blind users where passages of text or figures from a spreadsheet are spoken by the computer.

In addition, speech or voice input is a rapidly developing means of input to a computer. It is already an important method for people who are severely handicapped, or where the user's hands need to be free to do other things, but it requires fast processing and large amounts of memory. Programs are available which will recognise continuous speech input, translating the words directly into a word processor. Some words sound the same but are used in different contexts, eg 'weather' and 'whether' or 'sail' and 'sale'. These programs can select the appropriate spelling from the sentence that is spoken.

Speakers

All computers have a small built-in speaker to provide the basic sounds programmed in to various actions of the operating system, for example, the noises generated when the computer is switched on and off. For computers that require a higher quality of sound output, for example home microcomputers, separate speakers are needed. These are normally powered speakers that plug into the computer's sound card. These provide the high-quality stereo sound needed for speech, games and music including sound files on CD and DVD discs.

Switching

Earlier in this section (see page 23), we looked at how switches could be used as input devices. Computers can also output signals to switch equipment and machines on and off. This control of equipment requires much greater electrical power than can be provided by the computer. It is therefore necessary to boost the computer's signal with special power-switching electronic components.

Touch screen

On touch screens there are criss-crossing beams of infra-red light just in front of the glass on the computer monitor. When a user touches the glass with their finger, two sets of rays are blocked: the rays travelling from side to side and the rays going from top to bottom. The computer can detect the position of the finger from the light sensors placed on the opposite side of the monitor screen to the light sources, and respond accordingly. Touch screens are easy to use (user-friendly) and might be found as input devices in public places (eg museums) with information software.

Touch pad

A touch pad is a pressure-sensitive pad which provides input signals to the computer. A common form of touch pad, also known as a track pad, is found on notebook computers. The movement of the finger (or stylus) around the pad translates to the movement of the cursor on the screen, allowing the finger to become a pointing device.

Trackerball

A trackerball is similar to a mouse but the ball is set into a cup on the top of the unit. A finger or, on larger trackerballs the palm of the hand, is used to roll the ball in any direction. The ball controls the movement of the pointer on the screen. Buttons on the trackerball work in the same way as mouse buttons to activate processes on the screen.

Video digitiser

Digital camcorders can plug straight into computers via a Firewire interface. (A Firewire interface is the name given to a very fast data link between the computer and the digital camcorder.) This allows the computer to download, store and manipulate the digital video image.

Conventional camcorders can also transfer video into a computer, but because the image is held in analogue form, a video digitiser or video capture card is required to convert the signal into a digital format for storage and/or display on the computer (see pages 66 and 67 for information on analogue and digital formats).

Video capture and editing requires computers with large hard disk drives since files containing video data tend to be quite large. Captured files can then be edited in a number of ways, mixed together and compressed, to take up significantly less memory (as little as $^1/_{100}$ of the original size) with relatively low loss in image quality.

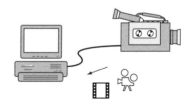

The human–computer interface

The way in which a computer user communicates with the computer is called the human–computer interface (or man–machine interface).

A good interface between the user and the computer program should be:

- **friendly** – being able to use the software without needing to read the whole manual first

- **attractive** – encourages users to use the software

- **effective** – it does the job it is designed to do efficiently

- **easy to use** – menu structures are consistent across packages (eg to save a program, users expect to find the option under the File drop-down menu).

Graphical user interface (GUI)

One form in common use is the graphical user interface or GUI system (pronounced 'Gooey'). Small pictures or icons representing actions are displayed and can be selected with the mouse. The use of windows makes the operation of programs easier.

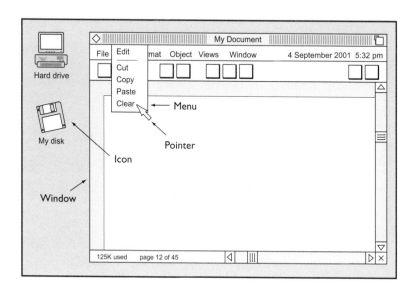

The screen may display several windows for different applications but only the one currently in use will be active. Another term used for this form of interface is WIMP (**w**indows, **i**cons, **m**enus and **p**ointer).

Command line interface

It is possible to give the computer instructions without the aid of menus and icons. This is done by typing the instructions directly into the computer so that they can be seen onscreen. This has the disadvantage that the user must know the commands to type in. The advantage is that quite specific instructions can be given directly.

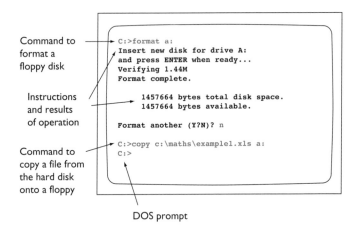

Command to
format a
floppy disk

Instructions
and results
of operation

Command to
copy a file from
the hard disk
onto a floppy

```
C:>format a:
Insert new disk for drive A:
and press ENTER when ready...
Verifying 1.44M
Format complete.

    1457664 bytes total disk space.
    1457664 bytes available.

Format another (Y?N)? n

C:>copy c:\maths\example1.xls a:
C:>
```

DOS prompt

Operating systems

All computers use an operating system (OS). This is a complex program which controls the entire operation of the computer. It handles input such as data from the keyboard and output to the screen and also the transfer of data to disk drives. A sophisticated OS can handle multiple processors, users and tasks simultaneously. Examples of three well-known operating systems are:

- **UNIX** – was written in the computing language C and is a multiuser, multitasking OS for microcomputers, minicomputers and mainframes.

- **Microsoft® Windows 95/98/Me** – is a popular operating system used in PCs in homes, schools and in businesses.

- **Microsoft® Windows NT/2000/XP** – is a more complex multitasking operating system for microcomputers, often used in network environments. If you are using Windows 95 or 98 on a school network then it is quite likely that the operating system being used by the network server(s) is a form of Windows NT.

Tasks of an operating system

Some of the tasks that an operating system needs to perform to ensure the efficient operation of the computer system include:

- allocating a slice of time with the processor for each job that needs to be processed

- ensuring that jobs with different priorities are dealt with in the correct order

- creating a balance between tasks which require a lot of processing time and tasks needing more use of peripherals like printers

- handling input and output and ensuring that input goes to the right program and output goes to the right place

- maximising use of the computer's memory by allocating different sections to the programs and data in use.

The development of Microsoft® Windows

The following is a summary of the development of Microsoft® Windows:

- **Windows 1/2** – These were early graphical user interfaces (GUI – see page 33) which Microsoft released in 1985 and 1987. They are almost never seen today.

- **Windows 3** – This family, which includes Windows 3.0, 3.1 and Windows for Workgroups, was released in 1990, and became the first successful version of Windows. It provides a GUI, and the ability to run several applications at once. Most software released since 1995 will not run on Windows 3, but it is still widely used throughout the world, particularly in large corporate companies where they do not feel it is necessary to upgrade to Windows 95/98. Microsoft no longer supports Windows 3. Sometimes Windows 3 is known as 16-bit Windows.

- **Windows 95/98/Me** – Windows 95 introduced many changes, including a redesigned graphical user interface, longer filenames, better multitasking and more support for networks and the Internet. More peripherals (such as printers, scanners, sound cards and CD drives) were supported. Windows 98 and Me are very similar to Windows 95, with easier Internet access and support for more peripherals. Nearly all currently available software will run on all of these versions of Windows.

- **Windows NT/2000/XP** – This is aimed at corporate users, and designed for more powerful computers. The graphical interface looks the same as Windows 95/98, but it is more reliable, although it does not support as wide a range of hardware. Most, but not all, software will run on Windows NT and 2000. Windows 2000 is very similar to Windows NT, but supports more hardware. The upcoming Windows XP is based on Windows 2000, but is aimed at current users of Windows 95/98/Me as well as NT/2000. Windows 95, 98, Me, NT, 2000 and XP are collectively known as 32-bit Windows.

- **Windows CE** – This is designed for palmtop computers and other small devices. It will not run software designed for Windows 95/98 or NT. Its user interface resembles Windows 95, but does not have as many functions. Cut-down versions of Microsoft® Word, Excel and Internet Explorer are available.

File types

When you create a document on a computer, for example in a word processing program, you can save it on disk in a file. Exactly what kind of information goes into the file often depends on the particular program that you use; so, for example, if you typed some text into Microsoft® Word and saved it into a file, you will not necessarily be able to open that file with WordPerfect.

To complicate matters further, there may be more than one version of a particular package. For example, if some text is typed into Word 2000 and saved, then it can be loaded into Word 97, but not Word 6/95.

Standard file formats

Standard file formats are one way of getting around these problems. Many programs will allow you to choose the format in which to save a file, the default being the proprietary format. In the above case, the document could be saved in RTF (rich text format), which is supported by most word processors, or 'text only', in which case any styles such as italics, fonts, etc, would be lost. In addition, many packages allow you to save files in a proprietary format readable by a previous version: in Microsoft® Word 97, for example, you can save a file in a format readable by Word 6/95 (but not necessarily by other word processing programs).

Filenames

The type of information a file contains, on many computers, is identified by the extension of the file's name. This is three characters that occur after a dot in the filename. For example, the extension for Microsoft® Word documents is DOC. On some computers, this is hidden; on others, you can see it.

Icons

On 32-bit Windows and on Apple Macintosh computers, the type of a file is also indicated by the icon used to represent it when browsing files on the disk.

For example, Microsoft® Word documents are indicated by an icon which looks like a piece of paper with a stylised letter W overlaid (see page 38). If you are given a file of a type your computer does not recognise, it may appear with a generic icon next to it. On 32-bit Windows, this looks like a piece of paper with a Microsoft® Windows logo on it; on Apple Macintosh computers, it looks like a plain piece of paper.

File formats

Some common file formats are described below:

Program files

On PCs, files containing programs you can run have the extension EXE, and may be intended for any of the Microsoft operating systems. If in doubt, try running the program; you will usually get a message if it is unsuitable for your computer.

Proprietary formats

These are formats for which you need a specific application to be able to read them. Each of these formats comes in several versions, depending on the version of the program used to save them:

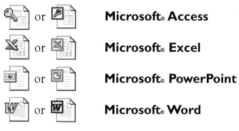

Microsoft® Access

Microsoft® Excel

Microsoft® PowerPoint

Microsoft® Word

 PDF

PDF stands for portable document format, and is a common way of distributing paper documents on disk and on the Internet. Its advantage is that the layout and appearance of documents is always preserved, regardless of the configuration of the computer on which they are viewed. Special software is needed to create files in PDF format, but they can be read with the Adobe Acrobat Reader application, which is free.

Standard datafile formats

These are formats which are readable by a number of different applications. If you want to provide a file for someone else and you are not sure what programs they have, or if you are having trouble saving a file and loading it into a different application, then try one of these formats:

- **Bitmap (.bmp)** – This is a standard file format for bitmap images, that is, images such as photographs rather than line drawings or charts.

- **Comma-separated values (.csv)** – If you save your spreadsheet in this format, you will be able to load it into another spreadsheet package or a database, but any formulae or graphs you have set up will be lost.

- **EPS (.eps)** – EPS stands for Encapsulated PostScript. This is a vector-image format and is most useful for illustrations and formatted pages from a desktop publishing package.

- **GIF (.gif)** – GIF stands for graphics interchange format, and is a standard format for images used in Web pages.

- **JPEG (.jpg)** – JPEG stands for joint photographic experts group, the name of the group of people who designed the format. It is a standard format used for images on Web pages, and is particularly well suited to photographs.

- **Rich text (.rtf)** – Saving in this format from your word processor will keep most styling, but may lose some features specific to your word processor, such as inserted pictures, special formulae, etc.

- **Text only (.txt)** – Saving in this format from your word processor will lose any styling you have set up, but will retain the raw text.

- **Tiff (.tif)** – This is similar to the bitmap format, except that it can contain additional information about the image.

- **Zip (.zip)** – Zip files contain one or more files in a compressed form, which take up less space than the separate files. This format is often used for files downloaded over the Internet, to save time when downloading. Using a suitable application, such as WinZip, you can extract the files from the zip file.

Communications

A vital part of Information and Communication Technology is for computers to send data to other computers, peripherals and control devices. There are a number of ways in which this data can travel:

Communication without cables

Infra-red

+   Freedom of movement for the machine
-   Must have direct line of sight
-   May be affected by strong sunlight

Wireless

Connecting a computer to a network using a wireless connection is becoming increasingly popular. A box with a wireless antenna is connected to the network and positioned in a area central to where the computers are to be used. Desktop and notebook computers are then fitted with wireless cards.

+   Can move around with a laptop
+   No need for fixed cables and sockets
-   Still quite low bandwidth (slow data transfer)
-   Limited range (approximately 100 m)
-   Signals absorbed by walls
-   Performance decreases as more computers used

The latest technology using short range radio waves, called Bluetooth, is being developed to link devices without the need for cables or 'line-of-sight' infra-red connections. It uses short range radio waves which can travel up to ten metres. Bluetooth applications include connecting the mouse and keyboard to computers, and wireless headsets to mobile phones.

Microwave

+   Secure data communication between remote sites
-   Direct line of sight required

Satellite

+   Communication between continents
-   Expensive to put satellites in orbit

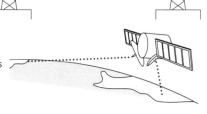

Satellites use a narrow, highly directional beam capable of many simultaneous transmissions. They are usually in an orbit such that their position above the Earth does not change (called a geostationary orbit).

Communication with cables

Wire cables

+ Cheap and easy to use
- Signal needs boosting over long distances

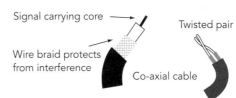

Signal carrying core

Wire braid protects from interference

Co-axial cable

Twisted pair

A common type of cable used for networking computers is called UTP cable. This is likely to be used for your school network and stands for unshielded twisted pair. The cable has eight wires that form four twisted pairs, each with its own colour code so that the network plugs and sockets can be wired correctly.

Fibre-optic cable

+ Can carry many signals at the same time
+ Free from electrical interference
+ Data is secure
+ Does not suffer from corrosion
- Equipment and cables are expensive

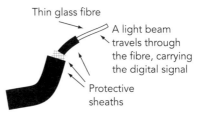

Thin glass fibre

A light beam travels through the fibre, carrying the digital signal

Protective sheaths

Data transmission rates

When considering the many forms of communicating data it is important to able to measure and compare the speed of transmissions. Baud is the unit used to measure serial transmissions of data.

One baud = One bit per second

A character in a computer is formed from eight bits so if we also include the 'start' bits, 'stop' bits and 'error' bits we can see how much data can be transferred from the baud rate. If we connect to the Internet at home using a modem (see page 47) then the standard baud rates are: 28.8 kbps (kilo bits per second), 33.6 kbps and 56 kbps. A typical data transmission rate for a school LAN (local area network – see page 43) is significantly higher at 100 000 kbps.

Data transmission

Fax

Fax is actually short for facsimile and is a way of sending documents over voice-quality telephone lines. A document is inserted into a fax machine and the telephone number of the receiving fax machine entered. The machine scans the document line by line and transmits these digital signals to the receiving fax, which then prints an identical copy of the document.

Telex

Telex is a well-established method of communication using the telephone network. Each telex subscriber is issued with a unique number which you often see printed on the letterheaded paper for businesses. To use telex you need a special keyboard and printer (monitors are not used). The message is typed on the keyboard and transmitted directly at slow speed to the receiving telex machine where the data is printed directly. No monitors are used with the system and no storage is available to hold messages.

An advantage of this system is that there is a permanent record of all communications but the system itself is greatly inferior to current email systems. In less developed countries, telex still plays a vital role in communications.

Networking

Local area networks (LANs)

Computer systems are networked when they are linked together. This linking can be through wire cables, fibre-optic cables, microwave links or satellite. When computer systems are linked on the same site, eg a school, this is called a local area network (LAN).

Server

A server is a powerful computer which holds software to run the network. It also holds the shared resources of the network like the users' files, software packages and printer queues.

The advantages of using a network computer are:

- Printers can be shared – individual stations do not need their own printer. When they print, the data is stored in a queue on the server. The data is then passed to the printer in turn.
- Programs can be shared – software packages are stored on the server and downloaded to workstations as requested.
- Data can be shared – database files stored in the server are available to users around the network; data from CD-ROMs and DVDs can also be shared.
- Users can communicate with others on the network, sending messages and sharing files.
- There is control over users' access rights to programs and data.

The disadvantages of using a network are:

- The cost of installing the equipment is greater.
- A network manager is often needed to run the system.
- If the server fails, all the workstations are affected.
- As data is shared there is a greater need for security.

Installing software

Computer software packages need to be installed on the network and made available to users at some, or all, of the workstations. This software may include application packages which can be used by all departments (eg word processing, database and spreadsheet packages) or it might be a very specific package for a particular department.

The computer programs that form the package are generally installed onto the network server rather than on the hard drive of every workstation. When users log onto the network and select the package icon with the mouse, a copy of the program files is passed to the user's workstation. The master copy of the package stored on the server is 'read-only'; this prevents users from changing or deleting files. Only the network manager, with the administrator password, has the authority to change files in this area of the file server.

Many packages allow users to save their work. When the package is installed onto the network server, the manager will ensure that the user files are directed to an area of the server's disk drives which does allow 'read/write' access to users.

Intranets

An intranet is a LAN where information is published using the same techniques as the Internet, but is only available locally, and not worldwide, as with the Internet. An intranet provides a convenient way of making things such as timetable details available.

Network topology

Network topology is the name given to the way in which the computers are connected in the network. Computers can be connected in a bus, star or ring network structure:

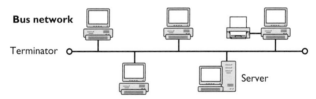

+ Easy and inexpensive to install (least amount of cable required)
− If the main cable fails, all the computers will be affected
− Performance of the network slows down with more users

Star network

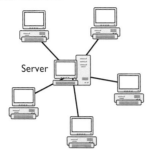

Server

Ring network

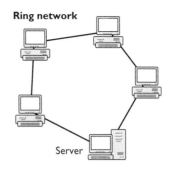

Server

+ Steady high performance, affected less by how many other computers on the network are being used	+ Data traffic between stations on the network is fast as it flows in one direction only
+ A cable failure does not affect other users	
− Uses a lot of cables which is expensive	− If the cable fails, all the stations are affected
− Requires a 'hub' box at the file server to control all the cables	

When using a computer on a network, it is necessary to 'log on' using a user name and password. The person responsible for looking after the network is called the network manager. They can give each user access to the particular programs and data they need.

Hubs and switches

A popular topology in schools is the star network. In the star topology, each computer has its own cable that leads back towards the network server. The server itself does not have sockets for all the cables to the workstations and so a hub unit is used. Hub units allow many workstations to be connected to the server and have multiple sockets called ports on the front panel. Hubs can be purchased with varying numbers of ports, eg 8, 12, 16 or 24 ports. In smaller schools, the computers are networked together without a server. This is called a peer-to-peer network and a hub unit is used to connect the workstations.

The illustrations below show how a hub can be used in these situations:

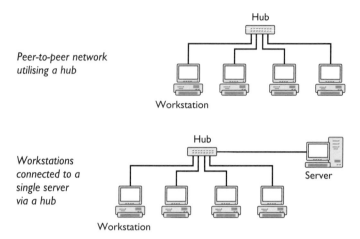

*Peer-to-peer network
utilising a hub*

*Workstations
connected to a
single server
via a hub*

On larger networks, devices called switches are used to connect servers and hubs together to form an integrated network. The illustration below shows a typical network topology for two servers and two hubs running many workstations:

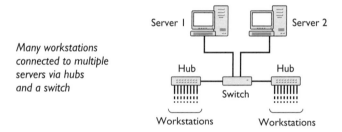

*Many workstations
connected to multiple
servers via hubs
and a switch*

Wide area networks (WANs)

When computers are linked over larger geographical areas, they form a wide area network (WAN). An example of a wide area network is the Internet (see page 49) which allows computer users to link to other computers around the world, often for the price of a local telephone call. To enable a computer to send and receive data using the telephone line, a modem, ISDN or DSL connection is required.

Modem

The word 'modem' is short for **mo**dulator **dem**odulator. Modems convert the digital signals in the computer to audio tones which can travel across the telephone system. It also converts incoming signals back into a digital form. The speed at which modems can transmit and receive data varies. The faster the modem, the quicker data transfers will be and lower telephone charges will result. A maximum speed for an Internet modem is 56 kbps (kilobits per second). Each character on the keyboard is made up of a code of eight bits. This means a modem working at this speed could receive over 6000 characters in a second.

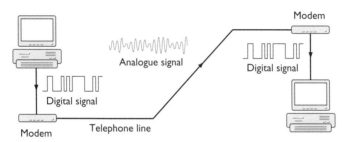

ISDN (integrated services digital network)

ISDN links share the same copper cable as an ordinary telephone but the computer data travelling along the wire is in digital form (1s and 0s). This means that there is no need for a modem to convert the signals into voice (analogue) waves. ISDN lines provide faster data transfer rates than ordinary telephone lines and transmissions are also more error-free. Typical data transfer speeds are 64 kbps in each direction. One noticeable difference in speed can be observed when connecting to the Internet; two to five seconds for ISDN rather than up to 30 seconds with a modem.

DSL (digital subscriber line)

DSL, like the ISDN line, uses the existing copper telephone lines but provides even faster data speeds. A common form of DSL is ADSL (asymmetric digital subscriber line). With ADSL, data is sent from the customer (home, school or business) to the Internet service provider at speeds of up to 640 kbps (typically 128 kbps). In the other direction, from the Internet to customer, data rates are typically 512 kbps to 1.5 Mbps (million bits per second). These speeds allow full multimedia access from the Internet including 'real-time' video, for example, movies on demand. In principle, DSL can reach higher speeds, up to 8 Mbps. Customers with DSL access are connected to the Internet 24 hours a day for a fixed monthly charge.

Broadband

Broadband is the name given to any data communication channel that has a wide bandwidth and can carry a large quantity of data. Under a recent government scheme, many of the schools in the UK are being connected to the Internet through broadband connections. This may vary from a dedicated 2 Mbps fibre-optic connection between the school and the Internet to shared access between a number of schools. DSL and cable modem technology are also classified as a broadband connection.

Cable

Some cable operators provide an Internet service over the same cables as they use for television. A special purpose cable modem is required. Like ADSL, the data transfer speed is typically different for data travelling from the Internet in to the customer and data travelling out from the customer. Incoming traffic is typically 512 kbps to 1.5 Mbps, while outgoing traffic is commonly limited to 128 kbps. In principle, speeds of up to 30 Mbps could be obtained. Customers with cable modem access are typically connected to the Internet 24 hours a day for a fixed monthly charge.

PSDN (public switched data network) and packet switching

An important development for the transmission of data around the UK is the PSDN. This network of cables, owned by BT and named Switchstream, is a packet switching network. Streams of data are chopped into small, manageable packets which, as well as the message portion, contain the destination address, source identification, the sequence number and error checking data. These packets travel from the source, across the network, often taking different routes. As the packets arrive at the destination, they are put back into the correct order using the packet sequence number. Transmission speeds are faster using the PSDN and modems are not required.

O Point of Presence (PoP) or network node

Packet switching

The Internet

The Internet is a huge international network made up of many smaller networks linked together like a spider's web. It started as a 'self-healing' communication system for the US government in case of nuclear disaster. It was then taken up by the academic community to exchange research material. It grew to include business and personal networks and is now a vast network spanning the globe.

The Internet is made possible by a collection of protocols which allow different computer systems to communicate with each other, regardless of the type of system being used. The main protocol which underpins the Internet is called TCP/IP (transmission control protocol/Internet protocol). Important protocols relying on TCP/IP include:

- SMTP (simple mail transfer protocol) – defines the way in which email (see page 51) is handled
- FTP (file transfer protocol) – enables users to transfer or download files to their computer
- HTTP (hypertext transfer protocol) – allows the browsing of World Wide Web pages (see page 54).

Connecting to the Internet

All that is required to use the Internet is:

- a computer
- a modem, ISDN connection or DSL
- communications software
- access to a local point of presence (PoP).

There are many organisations providing the link, or point of presence, where you dial in over the telephone (normally a local call) to make your connection to the Internet. These organisations, known as Internet service providers (ISPs), supply the communications software and may charge a small monthly subscription. Some major ISPs include BT Internet, Freeserve, Virgin, Tesco, CompuServe, Demon Internet, UK Online and AOL.

What the Internet provides

Using the Internet, it is possible to:

- send email
- join newsgroups or access bulletin boards
- access the World Wide Web
- trade via e-commerce (see below).

Information Superhighway

The Information Superhighway is the name given to the Internet now that the communication speeds are much higher. Fibre-optic cables and satellite links enable huge quantities of data to travel around the world and with broadband connections now reaching schools and businesses, the superhighway continues to grow.

e-commerce

e-commerce, also known as e-business, is the name given to trading over the Internet. This might be between one business and another, for example a manufacturer ordering materials, and is called B2B (business to business). Or it might involve using the Internet to sell to consumers, called B2C (business to consumer). Business on the Internet is rapidly changing the way in which we buy and sell goods and online trading is forecast to reach a trillion (1000 billion) pounds worldwide by 2003.

Email

Email, or electronic mail, is a way of sending messages, data, files or graphics to other users on the network. Subscribers to the Internet are given an email address, eg info@pearson.co.uk.

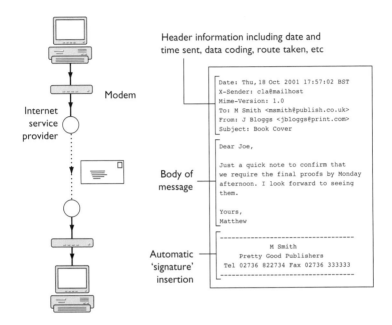

Email allows messages to be sent to anyone on the network, even on the other side of the world, for the price of the local telephone call. Hence, email is not free to the user but it is relatively cheap when compared with postal costs or a telephone call to another country, for example. When a message arrives, it is directed to the inbox of the user's mailbox. If they are not online when the message arrives, it is stored for them on the server of the user's ISP or on their company's mail server. Often, these messages only take minutes to travel around the world.

After reading this mail, the user can:

- delete the message
- file the message by storing it on disk
- send back a reply
- forward the message on to one or more other people.

Attachments

Sending plain text data in an email message is reasonably easy. It is also possible to send documents along with your message; these are known as attachments. There are a number of ways your attachment may be packaged up to send with your email by the software. Most modern email packages will now cope with any kind of attachment, but you may come across zipped files. It is common to compress files before emailing them so that they take up less space and hence take less time to arrive on your computer. The most common form of compression is zip; if you receive an attachment whose name ends in zip, then it is probably zip-compressed. You will need some software to 'un-zip' the file to retrieve the original (see file formats, page 38).

Care must be exercised with files attached to emails (or downloaded from the Internet or floppy disk) as they can contain computer viruses (see page 116). There have been many recent incidents of viruses being activated as attachments have been opened. For example, the Love Bug virus released in May 2000 spread rapidly around the world by emailing itself to the names in the address book of each user it reached. It also damaged files on the hard drive of the computer.

Bounced email

Just as the postal service is sometimes unable to deliver letters, so it is with email messages. If an email cannot be delivered, it will be returned to you, often with a rather cryptic message appended stating the nature of the error. Usually, a message is returned because the address is incorrect. It is important to get an email address exactly right; it must be spelled correctly and have the right punctuation. Email addresses are not usually case sensitive, but never contain spaces or commas, and always contain an @ symbol.

Email security

It is important to realise that email messages are not, in general, secure. It is very easy for malicious individuals to intercept an email message in transit and examine its contents, and it is also a simple matter for those with sufficient technical knowledge to forge an email from a particular person. In these respects, sending an email message is analogous to sending a postcard.

There are a number of software packages available, such as PGP (Pretty Good Privacy), which encrypt email messages before you send them, so that they cannot easily be read by anyone other than the intended recipient. Several email packages now support digital signatures, whereby an additional piece of data is added to each email message that you send which can be used to verify that an email really is from you.

Electronic bulletin boards

Electronic bulletin boards are an electronic form of a noticeboard. When users on the network visit the bulletin board site, they can read messages or leave their own for others to read. It is also possible to collect software programs from bulletin board areas. Usenet is one example of a bulletin board.

Usenet is a collection of newsgroups each on a single theme such as football, cooking or books. Each newsgroup contains postings from people – some providing information, some requesting information. When new announcements are made or queries asked, an ongoing discussion may start in the newsgroup. Nearly all Usenet newsgroups have FAQs (frequently asked questions) sections which hold answers to the most commonly asked questions. It is considered polite (or correct 'netiquette') for new users to read this information first before asking questions.

World Wide Web

Whilst the Internet is the physical network infrastructure, the World Wide Web is a multimedia retrieval system that runs on computers connected to the Internet, and is used to publish or access information. The Web gives businesses, schools and individuals access to a vast range of information resources. It is developing quickly and is changing the way we do many tasks. Shopping in cybermalls, banking and other customer services are available online, and many companies now use the Web as an essential means of communication between businesses that may be spread across the world. Satellite communications provide access to the Web where telephone or cable connection is not possible, thus opening up the entire globe. Hence, today we live in an Information Society, where access to and exchange of information are essential.

Using the Web

Uses of the Web include the following:

- finding information
- setting up a Web site
- arranging travel and accommodation
- buying goods
- managing bank accounts.

Finding information on the Web

To find information you could:

- enter the Web address (eg http://www.pearsonpublishing.co.uk/) or URL (uniform resource locator) of a Web site into your browser (see page 107)
- use an index, catalogue or jump list. Some Web sites have indexes or catalogues of other Web sites which may be specialised or attempt to cover the entire Web. Information can be found in these using techniques similar to searching the index in a book. A jump list is an index or catalogue where the entries are hyperlinks (ie highlighted text or graphics) to the information referred to
- use a search engine to look for information (see page 56)
- 'surf' the Web. This is when you use a browser to wander from one Web site to another by clicking on hyperlinks.

Setting up a Web site

The World Wide Web is what draws most people onto the Internet. It allows users to publish multimedia pages, containing text, graphics, sound and video information for users of the Internet to view.

Businesses, schools and individuals can make their own Web site pages incorporating text, graphics, digital sound and video. This can be done using special software like Microsoft® FrontPage 2000, using some desktop publishing packages, or by writing code, similar to programming. Different Web pages can be linked using hypertext hotlinks, in other words new pages are selected by clicking with the mouse on the linking text or graphics. Web pages are stored in a format known as HTML (hypertext mark-up language), an example of which is shown below:

```
<HTML>
    <HEAD>
        <TITLE>The Manor School</TITLE>
    </HEAD>
    <BODY>
        <CENTER>
            <H1>The Manor School</H1>
            <IMG SRC='schoollogo.gif'>
            <P>Welcome to our school's home page. Here at...
```

The Web browser interprets this text and displays the Web page. The <H1> tag, for example, tells it to display part of the text as a heading. Different Web browsers may display the page in slightly different ways; for example, if unspecified, the font size and face used may differ. More modern browsers allow you to use more complex layouts, but pages which include these features may not be readable by those with older software.

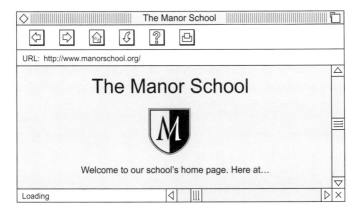

Search engines

If you know the address of a page on the Internet that you want to visit, then you can type it into your browser to go there. If, however, you don't know the address, or if you want to see if there is anywhere on the Internet that has information on a particular subject, then you should use a search engine.

Some examples are:

- AltaVista   http://www.altavista.com/
- Excite   http://www.excite.com/
- Galaxy   http://galaxy.com/
- Go.com   http://www.go.com/
- Google   http://www.google.co.uk/
- Lycos   http://www.lycos.co.uk/
- WebCrawler   http://www.webcrawler.com/
- Yahoo!   http://uk.yahoo.com/

Search engines provide 'fill-out' forms and other interfaces so the user can type in a query, submit the request, and retrieve a list of resources that match the search criteria. Results may vary from one search engine to the next.

Unfortunately, search engines are often not very good at filtering what they find and the user may have to scroll through many trivial or off-the-mark links before finding one that is useful. Each search engine has its own help button, and this might be explored to obviate the user spending hours seemingly getting nowhere!

Internet directories

Internet directories are collections of links to sites that have been organised by people under broad headings. You might try one of the huge Internet directories like Yahoo! or Galaxy. They are organised in topic sections which are clearly set out in hierarchies, or you can search using keywords. You could try both methods of searching – working down through the sections or using keyword searches.

Narrowing the search options

Most search engines and directories show you how to narrow down your search with a link to a page of tips. Read these before you start searching. You need to think carefully about what keywords you will use and how to combine them.

Bookmarks

Having discovered the really useful sites, you need to make a permanent note of them so that you don't have to go searching for them again. Your Web browser should be able to save bookmarks (or favourites) of these Web site addresses so that you can return to them easily at a future date.

Supervising access to the Web

There is an enormous amount of useful material available on the World Wide Web, but also much that is potentially harmful, especially to children. As well as pornographic Web sites, there are sites which give details on how to make bombs and some published by extreme right-wing racist groups. Giving unsupervised, unrestricted access to the Web to students is thus not a good idea, as even if children are not specifically looking for particular material, it is quite easy to stumble across it accidentally.

Software packages are available which block access to undesirable content, normally using one or a number of the following approaches:

- **Keyword matching** – The software searches in the text of each Web page viewed. If a keyword is found, access to the page is denied. The obvious drawback is that images are not checked, and that some sites which are harmless are blocked because they contain a particular keyword in a non-harmful context.

- **Prescribed Web sites** – The software has a list of Web sites which are allowed to be viewed; access to any site not on the list is denied. Although this method has the disadvantage that new Web sites need to added to the list before they can be viewed, it is probably the most secure way of stopping access to undesirable information. An example of this type of software is Net Nanny.

- **Proscribed Web sites** – The software has a list of 'banned' Web sites, to which access it denied. The problem with this approach is that new sites that appear will not be on the list, which must be constantly updated to ensure that all unwanted Web sites are listed.

Security

An increasing number of sites on the Web allow you to buy goods online. Some of them may ask you to type in your credit card details. Care should be taken in these circumstances, as you should only send such details over a secure connection, which is where information transmitted and received over the Internet is encrypted so that other people cannot read it. Usually, your browser will give some indication that this is the case; it may produce a pop-up message, or an icon may appear at the edge of the browser window.

Downloading files

As well as viewing Web pages, the Web allows you to download files to your computer. These may contain computer programs, such as shareware, or documents of another sort. Be aware that if you download a program from the Internet and run it, you risk transmitting a computer virus to your computer (see page 116). Check where the program comes from, and install virus checking software on your computer.

Some types of files you download may be associated with a program on your computer, in which case the browser will often start that program automatically once the file has downloaded, and use it to open the file. Sometimes this is not what you want to happen, and you can usually force the browser just to save the file to your computer's hard disk by clicking on the download link with the right-hand mouse button to call up a menu that allows you to do so.

Video conferencing

The term video conferencing refers to users communicating across networks using audio and video images. It is ideal for meetings between remote sites or different countries around the world where traditional meetings would involve considerable time and expense in travel and accommodation.

A camera, often placed on the top of the monitor, records the digital images of the user while a microphone captures the speech. These signals are then transmitted across the network to the receiving station where the image is displayed in a window on the monitor. In addition to the audio and video signals, data from applications can also be transmitted. For example, if a user is demonstrating using graphs from data in a spreadsheet then this could also be transmitted.

Video images generate large quantities of data and so it is necessary to compress the data and transmit it across high-speed channels. One method of compressing data is by using a codec card in the PC. The codec hardware compresses the data leaving the computer and decompresses the data arriving at the computer. The speed of data transmission across telephone lines using modems is not really fast enough for effective transmission. It is necessary to use ISDN lines, DSL or other broadband connections to obtain the necessary transmission rates (see pages 46 and 47).

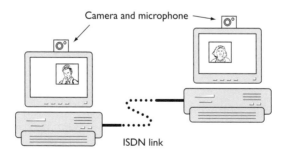

Camera and microphone

ISDN link

A simple video conferencing set-up

Standards and software

For one person to communicate with another person using video conferencing, both users must be using hardware and software that is compatible. This is achieved through internationally agreed standards which define how the video and audio data are compressed, how the data is transmitted and how it is shared. NetMeeting, supplied free with Windows 95/98/2000 is an example of software which complies with these standards.

Video conferencing installations

Depending on the number of people involved at each end of the video conferencing link, the arrangement of cameras and the size of the display screen will vary. Conferencing systems can be broadly divided into three groups as follows:

- **Desktop systems** – These are the simplest and least expensive systems to set up and are designed for single users.

- **Mobile units** – These video conferencing systems are installed on trolleys using larger display monitors more suited to use with small groups, up to around ten users. Mobile units are ideal for moving between classrooms in schools.

- **Room installations** – Equipping a room with video conferencing facilities to handle larger groups (eg 30 users) requires more sophisticated and expensive equipment. Several microphones will be necessary in the room and the camera needs to be voice-activated or manually controlled by a 'director' to point to the speaker. Large display units or projection systems are used to show the video and data being transmitted.

Benefits

There are various benefits to using video conferencing. For example, students can attend courses remotely, particularly when the school or college they attend cannot offer the course they want. Pupils taking Modern Foreign Language courses can interact directly with schools in other countries. Pupils can use the global Internet links to experience different cultures. Secondary schools can link directly with junior school classes to help bridge the transition for the younger pupils.

Computer control

Computers are now used to control the operation of many machines and everyday objects. The instructions contained in the computer program send signals out of the computer to devices like switches and motors which make the machine operate in the correct way.

Example of a control program

One programming language used to control the movements of a simple object is Logo. This language was designed for pupils in junior schools and can make a mechanical 'turtle' move around the floor on a sheet of paper (or an image onscreen). The turtle has a pen which can be lowered onto the paper so that a trail is left as the turtle moves across the paper. Some of the instructions from Logo are shown below:

FORWARD n	Move 'n' steps forward
BACKWARD n	Move 'n' steps backward
RIGHT d	Turn 'd' degrees to the right
LEFT d	Turn 'd' degrees to the left
PENUP	Lift the pen off the paper
PENDOWN	Lower the pen down onto the paper

To draw a square (size 50 units) and a hexagon (size 30 units) on the paper, we would program in the following instructions:

Square	**Hexagon** (6 sides)
PENDOWN	PENDOWN
FORWARD 50	FORWARD 30
RIGHT 90	RIGHT 60
FORWARD 50	FORWARD 30
RIGHT 90	RIGHT 60
FORWARD 50	FORWARD 30
RIGHT 90	RIGHT 60
FORWARD 50	FORWARD 30
PENUP	RIGHT 60
	FORWARD 30
	RIGHT 60
	FORWARD 30
	PENUP

These short programs contain several sets of repeated instructions. The program code can be shortened by using another Logo instruction:

REPEAT x [instruction]

This repeats the instructions in the brackets 'x' times.

The programs could now be written as shown below:

Square
```
PENDOWN
REPEAT 4 [FORWARD 50 RIGHT 90]
PENUP
```

Hexagon
```
PENDOWN
REPEAT 6 [FORWARD 30 RIGHT 60]
PENUP
```

When a computer is used to control machines, it is often necessary to input data from both the machines and the surrounding environment.

Feedback

Feedback is a term used in computer control when data input from a sensor causes the control program to make changes by sending signals to output devices. These changes are then recorded by the input sensor and data signals sent back to the computer. This process forms a loop as illustrated in the example below:

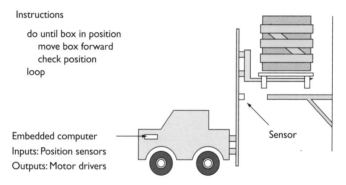

Instructions

    do until box in position
      move box forward
      check position
    loop

Embedded computer
Inputs: Position sensors
Outputs: Motor drivers

Sensor

Machine putting a box onto a shelf in a warehouse

Embedded computers

When a computer is used to control a machine, the computer circuit board is installed inside the machine. The input sensors and output control devices are then connected to these circuits. This is an embedded computer. The input/output devices that we are most familiar with – the keyboard, mouse, monitor and disk drive – are not required.

The computer control program is written using a 'normal' computer and 'downloaded' into the embedded computer. The software program is stored in a ROM (read only memory) chip and activates when the machine is switched on.

Using computers for control

The benefits of using computers for control are as follows:

- Although the cost of computerised machines in factories is high, the operating costs are low in comparison to wages for people doing the job.
- Computers work without the need for breaks and sleep.
- The quality of output from the machine is consistent.
- Machines can handle very heavy work or very precise tasks.
- Machines can work in places that are uncomfortable or hostile for people.
- Computers process data very quickly and so the machines can operate faster.
- Computers can operate the machines with data from a range of sources.

Applications

Some common applications of using computers for control are as follows:

Central heating controllers

Inputs: Switches on key pad.

Process: Mainly timing functions, storing several on/off settings for each day.

Outputs: Switches to turn the boiler on/off, to operate pumps and solenoids to control valves in the pipes.

More sophisticated controllers monitor whether a room is in use and switch off the heating in unused rooms. These controllers have the facility to 'learn' and can establish patterns of movement in the house. For example, if a person normally goes to bed at around 10.30 pm each night, the controller will detect this and switch the heating on in the bedroom just before this time.

Washing machines

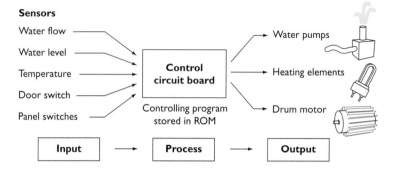

Sensors

Water flow ──→
Water level ──→
Temperature ──→
Door switch ──→
Panel switches ──→

Control circuit board

Controlling program stored in ROM

→ Water pumps
→ Heating elements
→ Drum motor

Input	→	Process	→	Output

Inputs: Water flow sensors, water level sensors, temperature sensors, panel switches, door open switch, spin speed selector.

Process: Stored programs for different wash cycles, eg woollens, cotton, etc. Each program controls the water temperature and level, and the timing and sequence of the wash, rinse and spin cycles.

Outputs: Switches to operate water pumps and valves, water heaters and the drum motor.

Camera

Inputs: Light sensor, push buttons, film speed sensor, battery power and end of film sensor.

Process: Calculate light level and adjust shutter speed and aperture according to film speed. Focus the lens to produce a sharp image. Activate motor to wind film on and draw back shutter for the next picture. Activate flash if necessary.

Outputs: Shutter release switch, motor on/off switch, flash.

Video recorders

Inputs: Switches on the control panel, infra-red detector for remote key pad, switches to detect whether the video tape is in the machine and the tape's recording/play back time.

Process: Timer and clock for switching the recorder on/off, memory to hold different recording dates and times, automatic scanning to find television channels.

Outputs: LCD display on front panel, switches to operate video tape drive motors.

Data logging

Data logging can be defined as the capture and storage of data for use at a later time. Sensors are used to input the data which is stored in memory. This data can then be displayed in graphs and tables, passed to a spreadsheet program for analysis, and printed and saved on computer disk. Data logging is particularly important in scientific experiments.

Sensors

Almost all physical properties can be measured with sensors. There are sensors to measure light, heat, sound, movement, pressure, strains and stresses in materials, acidity, humidity and radiation.

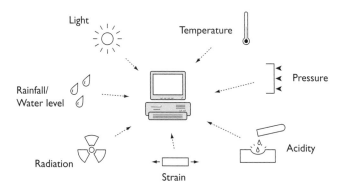

When an experiment is taking place in the laboratory, it is possible to link sensors directly through their control boxes to the computer. If we wish to record data out in the field, equipment would be needed that could measure and store data until the unit is brought to a computer and the data downloaded. Where the recording was taking place would determine how robust the data logging equipment would have to be.

Using data logging equipment for experiments

There are a number of advantages in using data logging in experiments. These include:

- Data loggers can record measurements with great accuracy.

- Sometimes the very act of taking a reading may interfere with the experiment, eg inserting a thermometer in a liquid may cool the liquid a fraction and also allow heat to escape through a lid. Sensors can be sealed inside the equipment.

- Data loggers can collect data measurements over very short or very long periods of time. For example, equipment could record and process hundreds of measurements during a chemical reaction lasting less than a second. Alternatively, it could be set to record the growth of a plant by taking measurements every hour, day and night, for months or even years.

- Data logging equipment can work reliably and consistently for long periods of time. People would need to take breaks to eat and sleep and, when tired, their efficiency may be reduced.

- Data loggers can operate in environments which would be hostile to people. Equipment can be designed to operate in orbiting satellites, the depths of the oceans, deserts, the Arctic or Antarctic.

Analogue and digital

A digital signal consists of pulses of electricity passing along a wire or track of a circuit board. At any point in the signal, there are only two states, either a pulse of electricity is present or there is no pulse. There is no in-between state.

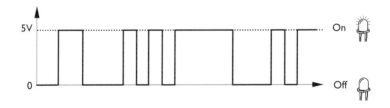

Computers operate using digital signals and all the data and program instructions are coded with different combinations of 1s and 0s.

Many sensors which are used to input data into computers produce analogue signals. Take, for example, a light-dependent resistor (LDR) sensor which reacts to the amount of light falling on it. The resistance to the flow of electricity through the device gets less as the light becomes brighter.

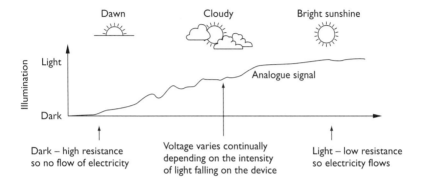

Because computers only work with digital signals, the analogue signals from the sensor must be converted to digital signals. This is done by an electronic device called an 'analogue to digital converter' (or 'A to D converter' for short). The varying voltage of the analogue signal is converted into pulses.

Sometimes it is necessary to reverse this process and take the digital signal from the computer to an output device that needs an analogue signal. In this case a 'digital to analogue converter' (or 'D to A converter') is used.

For example, the audio signal that travels along the telephone wire is analogue. A modem (see page 47) is both an 'A to D converter' and a 'D to A converter'. When connecting a computer to the Internet using telephone cables, the modem converts the incoming signals to digital for the computer and the outgoing signals from the computer to analogue to travel along the wires.

Computer aided design/manufacture

Computer aided design (CAD)

CAD packages are used by scientists, engineers and designers to design many things including cars, bridges, ships, circuit boards, computers, chemical plants, oil rigs and buildings. The software needed is often complex and requires powerful computers to run it. It is likely to have many special features, including:

- allowing the designer to draw an object in two dimensions (flat) and then having the software build and display a three-dimensional solid version of the design
- allowing the object to be rotated and viewed from different angles
- 'suggesting' suitable materials for constructing the objects, eg materials with sufficient strength or flexibility
- calculating the stresses and strains that a structure will have to withstand and, where necessary, give warnings of designs that are not safe
- simulating and testing the finished design, eg where CAD is used to design an electronic circuit, it can simulate the operation of the circuit.

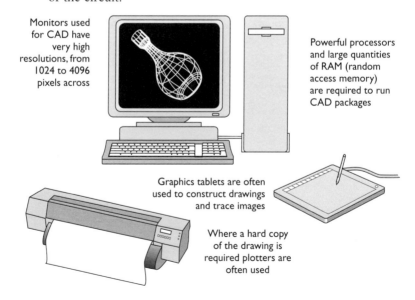

Monitors used for CAD have very high resolutions, from 1024 to 4096 pixels across

Powerful processors and large quantities of RAM (random access memory) are required to run CAD packages

Graphics tablets are often used to construct drawings and trace images

Where a hard copy of the drawing is required plotters are often used

Using CAD software enables drawings to be done more quickly. Changes can be made without having to start the whole drawing again and parts of drawings which are needed more than once can be copied and then duplicated as many times as required. Many companies have large libraries of drawings held on disk which can be retrieved and modified very rapidly. Very fine detail can be achieved by zooming in on the drawing, and many of the tedious tasks of hatching and shading areas can be done automatically by the computer.

Using a computer network, a number of designers can work on the same project at the same time and workers throughout the company, from the board room to the shop floor, can access drawings on their terminals to assist them with their work and decision making.

Computer aided design software is not just a drawing package. It can be sophisticated software that can calculate, from the dimensions of the drawing, the weight, strains and the stresses that the finished object will endure. In this way, weakness in structures like bridges can be avoided. When using CAD software to design electronic circuits, the software can simulate voltages to test the circuit even before it has been constructed.

Computer aided manufacture (CAM)

Computer aided manufacture is a process of aiding production in manufacturing companies by using computers to operate machines. Some machines shape materials; three of the more common processes are lathing, milling and drilling:

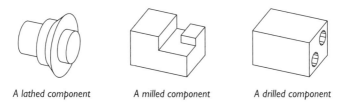

A lathed component   A milled component   A drilled component

Other machines transport the goods between one process and the next, and computer-controlled robot arms may be involved in spraying paint or welding joints.

CAD/CAM

The most effective method of production is to design products using a computer aided design package and then pass instructions directly from this package to the machines able to manufacture the product. Data from the design software is translated into instructions for guiding the lathes, milling and drilling machines. The whole process is fully automated. The introduction of these systems into manufacturing industry has:

- increased production – machines do not need breaks or sleep
- dramatically reduced the numbers of workers
- reduced the demand for machine operators
- created the demand for skilled computer operators.

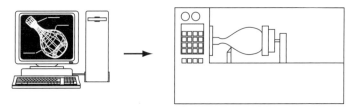

Product is designed on CAD system, the data is transferred to computer numeric control (CNC) machines, and the product manufactured with CAM

Modelling and simulation

Modelling

Modelling is when a computer program attempts to represent a real situation. In order to do this, mathematical equations are used, but the accuracy of the computer model depends on how well the 'real' process is understood. Different values can be input to the model to investigate possible outcomes. A spreadsheet can be used as a modelling program.

Modelling example

The illustration below shows how a modelling program could also be designed to assist in the construction of a flood protection scheme:

The computer model can experiment with different flood protection barriers of varying lengths, heights and positions to find the most effective and lowest cost protection system

The height of tides, the effects of air pressure and the effect of global warming on the sea level can be modelled by the computer and used as inputs to the program. The computer program can calculate the volume and flow of water based on these inputs

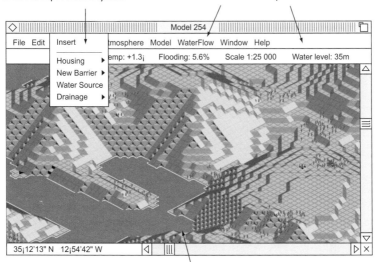

The land levels, natural barriers and water movements can be built into the model

Simulation

A simulation program is designed to predict the likely behaviour of a real-life system. The real-life situation is represented as a mathematical model in the computer program. Simulation packages include flight simulators and weather forecasting.

Computer simulation example

Modern flight simulators used for training pilots are full-size cockpits mounted on hydraulic arms to give a full range of movement. Computer screens are positioned in place of windows and these display lifelike images which change according to movement of the aircraft through the controls.

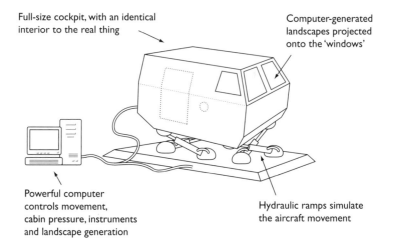

Full-size cockpit, with an identical interior to the real thing

Computer-generated landscapes projected onto the 'windows'

Powerful computer controls movement, cabin pressure, instruments and landscape generation

Hydraulic ramps simulate the aircraft movement

To be able to train a pilot in a lifelike simulator without leaving the ground can have a number of advantages. These include:

- the simulator is less expensive to operate than an actual aeroplane
- pilot training is not affected by weather conditions
- training in emergency situations can be safely given
- different conditions such as night flying can be simulated
- practice can be give for take-off and landing at airports worldwide at the press of a button.

Software

Software is the general name for programs that are suitable for a range of purposes, from writing a letter to controlling a set of traffic lights. Here are some software applications that are widely used in the home, in schools and in business:

- word processors – used to produce letters, reports, projects
- computer graphics – used to create and edit images
- desktop publishing packages – used to design books, leaflets, advertisements, posters
- databases – used to store, sort, search and retrieve information
- spreadsheets – used for calculations, forecasting and modelling
- presentation graphics – used for preparing and delivering a presentation onscreen
- multimedia – used to find information
- Web browsers – used to explore the World Wide Web.

Example of software use

The illustration below shows how a uniform shop in a school might use four software packages:

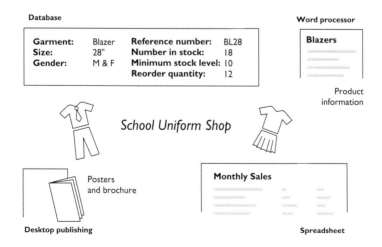

The uniform shop needs to purchase the different clothes (blazers, shirts, trousers, ties, sportswear, etc) from the manufacturers. A database is kept of all the goods held in the uniform shop including the type of garment, the size and the number in stock. This helps to:

- monitor stock levels and print out reports
- reorder new stock before items run out of stock
- search the database for items of uniform when parents enquire.

The school may wish to make a small profit from the shop and so a spreadsheet is used to calculate the selling price for each item, also the monthly and yearly sales figures. A word processor is used to write letters to parents, place orders with the suppliers and prepare the price lists each term. The desktop publishing package is used to produce posters advertising the uniform shop, and the days and times it opens.

Software features

The clipboard

One important feature of using software packages is the ability to cut (or copy) and paste between packages. The sections of work that have been selected (highlighted) can be cut or copied and then pasted into another position in the document, into another document or into another software package.

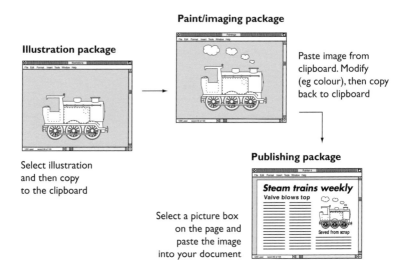

Paint/imaging package

Illustration package

Paste image from clipboard. Modify (eg colour), then copy back to clipboard

Select illustration and then copy to the clipboard

Publishing package

Steam trains weekly
Valve blows top

Saved from scrap

Select a picture box on the page and paste the image into your document

When the cut or copy option is used, the selected material is held in a part of the memory referred to as the 'clipboard'. Only one selection can be held in the clipboard at a time, so if another cut or copy is done the first selection is lost from the clipboard.

Macros

A macro is a way of recording and storing a sequence of keystrokes or instructions. These can then be 'played back' when required by running the stored macro. A macro facility can often be found in most software packages and can help to reduce the time taken for repetitive tasks or help the user to perform more complex instructions. For example, a macro might be set up in a:

- word processor – to insert your details at the top of a page
- database – to carry out instructions to search for certain records, sort them into order and then print the records out
- spreadsheet – to draw a graph of some results.

Once a macro has been recorded, it is given a name and stored. It can then be activated by a combination of key presses (known as hot keys), eg CTRL + J or by placing a button on the screen.

Word processing

A word processor can be used to write letters, reports, essays, projects, memos, curriculum vitae, theses – in fact, any form of written work. When text is entered at the keyboard, the characters and words are displayed on the screen and held in the computer's memory. This work can be saved to disk and printed.

The advantage of using a word processor is that the text can be changed (edited) onscreen and reprinted if mistakes are made. The word processor also has many features which can be used to format the document.

Formatting

When we format a document we choose the way it looks. Characters can be **bold**, *italic*, <u>underlined</u> or CAPITAL letters. The spacing between letters and lines can be altered or the writing can be set out in columns or tables.

Bold
Emboldening titles, sub-titles, words or phrases will make them stand out.

Columns
Text can be placed in columns like those of a newspaper.

Bullets
Bullets are used to highlight a series of statements or a list in the document. The most common bullet is the filled circle.

Fonts

Font is the name we give to a style of print. There are many different fonts. Two quite common ones are Times and Helvetica:

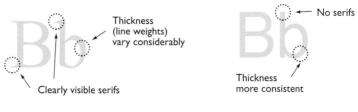

Times – A serif font

Helvetica – A sans serif font

Fonts can be broadly grouped into serif and sans serif fonts. Serifs on a character are the cross-strokes that cap the strokes which make up a character. In the illustration above you will see that the Times font has serifs but the Helvetica font does not. Serifs help the eye flow along the line as the words are read and serif fonts are often used in newspapers and magazines. Sans serif fonts can be used on application forms, for example, where the eye of the reader needs to be drawn to each box in turn.

Justification

There are four ways in which text can lie in a column and at any stage the user can alter all or part of the document to any one of the four.

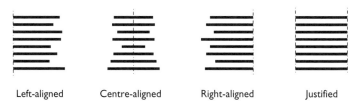

| Left-aligned | Centre-aligned | Right-aligned | Justified |

For justification, where the text is lined up to both the left- and right-hand edges, the program checks, line by line, the length of the text. If it is less than the line length, it stretches the text by spreading the letters and words, or by inserting additional spaces between words.

Tabs

Tabs are often used for setting out tables or columns. Tab positions can be set across the page. Then, when the tab key on the keyboard is pressed, the cursor (flashing bar) will jump to the next tab position across the page.

The four most common types of tab markers: left, right, centre and decimal are shown below:

Centre tab	Left tab	Right tab	Decimal tab
↓	↳	↰	↓
Resistor	0.22 ohms	6z – 0100	£0.12
Capacitor	56 pF	08 – 0495	£0.07
Relay	5V DC 80R	60 – 585	£1.10
Semiconductor	3A+5V	LM 323 K	£2.40
Tools	Precision Drill	85 – 55	£29.70

Setting up a page

Landscape or portrait

Ordinary A4 paper (29.7 cm x 21 cm) can be printed in two orientations, known as portrait and landscape. Portrait is printed with the longest side vertical, this is the usual (default) setting. Alternatively, landscape can be selected which prints with the longest side horizontally. Landscape orientation can be useful when designing an A5 booklet where the A4 page will be folded, or for wide tables, illustrations and use of columns.

Headers

Headers allow the user to specify text which will automatically be printed at the top of each page. The position across the page, and the style and size of the header text, can be specified. Items that might be placed in a header include the description of the document or the chapter number.

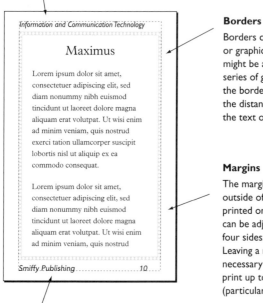

Borders

Borders can be placed around text or graphics in a document. A border might be a single line, double line or a series of graphic images. The size of the borders can be altered as well as the distance between the border and the text or graphic inside.

Margins

The margin is the area around the outside of the paper which is not printed on. The sizes of the margins can be adjusted individually for the four sides: top, right, left and bottom. Leaving a margin on the page is necessary as many printers cannot print up to the edge of the paper (particularly the bottom edge).

Footers

A footer, as the name implies, is found at the foot of the page. As with headers, once the layout of a footer is defined for all or part of a document, it will appear on each printed page. The footer often contains the page number which is automatically increased through the document.

Style sheets

A style sheet holds information about the parts of a document: the body of the text, chapter titles, headings and subheadings, footers and headers, etc. Each style sheet might contain information on the font to be used, the size, alignment, spacings, colour, background, border, shading, etc. Once style sheets have been set up for a document, they are very easy to apply; highlight the particular text, eg a heading, then select the heading style from the menu list. The advantages of using style sheets in documents are:

- it is quick to apply a range of formatting to the highlighted text
- with long documents it makes it easy to be consistent, ie all the titles, subtitles, etc having the same style throughout the document
- marking text with the heading style will allow the word processor to automatically create a 'contents' page in longer documents
- it makes it very easy to change formats throughout the whole document.

Editing

Spell-check

The spell-check facility makes use of an extensive dictionary held on the disk. Each word in your document is compared with words in the dictionary and the user is invited to change or ignore words selected by the spell-checker. When words in the document are not found in the dictionary, the spell-checker will suggest words that have similar spellings or that sound similar when spoken.

Often spell-checkers have the facility to create dictionaries for the user for special words. These words might include real names, address names, postcodes and technical words not normally found in a dictionary. Dictionaries are also available for specialist subjects like medicine.

Grammar check

The grammar check will look at the way each sentence in the document is written and compare it with a set of rules for grammar and style of writing. The user can usually select how strictly these rules are applied to their work. The grammar check will suggest ways in which the sentence can be improved if it varies from the rules. The check often includes statistics on readability: based on the number of syllables in words, the length of words and the number of words in sentences, the reading age can be determined. 'Standard' writing averages 17 words per sentence and 147 syllables per 100 words.

Many modern word processors check the spelling and grammar as the words are entered, indicating errors with coloured lines.

Thesaurus

Select a word, or phrase, and the thesaurus will display a range of words with the same or similar meanings.

Mailmerge

The diagram below illustrates the process of a mailmerge operation. This is often used to produce personalised letters and is achieved by having a standard letter containing fields that pull in data from a separate source. The data source could be a table in a word processor, cells from a spreadsheet or, most commonly, records in a database. When the mailmerge is started, the data replaces the fields in the standard letter. A letter is produced for every database record or row of a table.

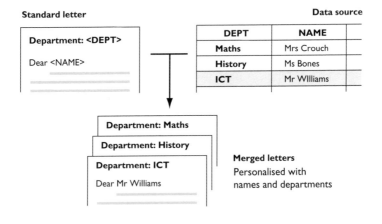

Computer graphics

Generating graphics on the computer has many different and important uses. Drawing and painting packages can be used by illustrators to create images, and games programmers use graphics extensively to produce fast and exciting animations. Many of the special effects seen on television have been generated through computer graphics, and computer aided design (CAD) is vital for many businesses (see page 68).

Clip art

Programs like the Microsoft® Office collection, come with their own library of professionally-prepared graphics for use in documents and publications. CDs and DVDs can also be purchased containing different clip art pictures. Alternatively, images can be downloaded from Web sites offering free clip art.

Input devices used with drawing and painting packages are the mouse, scanners (digitisers) and graphics tablets.

Painting packages

Painting programs such as Microsoft® Paint which comes with Microsoft® Windows, are always popular. Paint programs are usually raster graphics packages where the image is held as a bitmap. The picture is made up of tiny picture elements called pixels. When you zoom into a bitmap image, the edges are jagged. Bitmap images take up a lot of computer memory as even the blank parts of the picture are stored.

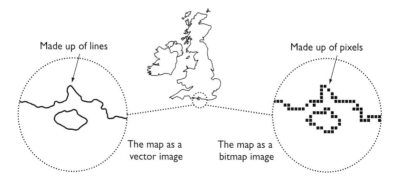

Made up of lines

Made up of pixels

The map as a vector image

The map as a bitmap image

Illustration packages

Drawing programs, like Microsoft® Draw, use vector graphics. This means that the shapes which are drawn are stored in memory as a series of instructions. This has two main advantages:

- they take up less memory – often a small fraction of the size of a similar bitmap image
- scaling the images does not result in a loss of quality. An image scaled by 1000% will have just as smooth lines when printed as the non-scaled version.

With an illustration package, you can easily:

- fill and stroke shapes with colour
- draw and edit regular or freehand shapes
- draw smooth, irregular curves
- scale, shear, rotate and flip shapes
- create complex shapes and masks
- edit text character shapes
- duplicate shapes quickly.

An image created using an illustration package

Modern illustration packages have many more complex functions available to the user, which include:

- sophisticated blending one shape into another
- enhanced typographic controls
- converting 2-D images into 3-D representations
- complex gradiated colour fills.

Photographic editing packages

Photographic editing packages are used to edit photographic images, once they have been scanned using a scanner, or captured using a digital camera or video camera. They are used extensively in publishing and allow the user to:

- rotate, shear, scale and crop an image
- merge several images to make a complex image (by joining them edge to edge, by fading one into another or by overlaying them transparently)
- edit images (ie remove backgrounds)
- adjust the colour balance
- add or remove colour
- sharpen or blur the image
- apply filters to change the style of an image (ie to make a photograph look like an impressionist painting)
- apply noise or textures to an image.

In addition, they often have many painting functions available to the user (pencils, paintbrush, airbrush, etc).

Photographic images, like painted images, are stored as bitmap images, and as such can be quite large. For example, a single full page A4 image used in a magazine might have a file size of 30 MB or more.

Resolution

Resolution is a measure of how much detail is able to be held in an image file. It is measured in dots per inch (dpi). As the name suggests, this is the number of pixels per linear inch, if it is not scaled. A good resolution for printing from ink-jet printers is 150 dpi. Even this, however, will result in file sizes of several megabytes for an A4 page.

Scaling bitmap images

When bitmap images are scaled, the resolution is scaled also. For example, if you have a photograph 6 cm by 4 cm, and you want to scan it and print it using an ink-jet printer at twice the size, then the image needs to be scanned at twice the ouput resolution (ie 300 dpi). Scaling the image by 200% reduces the resolution proportionately, and this needs to be taken into account when scanning.

Editing functions

Here is an example of some of the common editing functions of graphics packages:

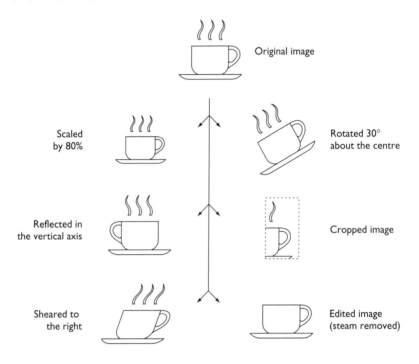

Layers

When pictures are positioned over text or text is placed over pictures in a document, this is called layering. In order to create the effect required, it may be necessary to select the object and 'Send to back' or 'Bring to front'. It is also possible to make the text background transparent so that the picture or image can be seen behind the text.

Objects in layers can be moved 'on top' of each other

Desktop publishing (DTP)

A desktop publishing (DTP) program allows users to look at a page of a document as a whole and design the layout by marking areas for text and graphics. Although many modern word processors have a lot of the features found in desktop publishing packages, they can be slow and cumbersome to use.

Desktop publishing packages are designed for laying out text and graphics on a page, and for these tasks they are quick and easy to use. Pages can be laid out in complex ways, with text arranged in columns with large titles or headlines heading the columns, and text flowing round placed images. Images can be imported from graphics packages, scanned, digitised or taken from clip art libraries on disk or CD-ROM.

In addition, they have sophisticated typographic control (the way the text is handled) and style sheets (see page 78). As well as defining paragraph attributes, style sheets can be created to control individual words or sentences. The user has tight control over:

- type font, size, style and weight
- leading (the spacing between lines)
- tracking and kerning (the spacing between characters)
- paragraph spacing, indentation, drop caps
- rules and tabs.

DTP can be used to produce newspapers, newsletters, books, posters, brochures, leaflets, prospectuses, packaging, etc.

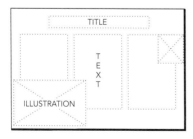

Design

Finished page

Graphics

Documents often require graphics, such as pictures and images, to illustrate the text. These can be obtained from:

- clip art or image libraries
- drawing and painting packages
- scanners, digitisers and digital cameras.

Once inserted, DTP packages allow the user to flow text around the images in numerous ways:

Text can flow around the image bounding box...	...which can also be circular, or almost any shape.	The text can be in more than one column...	...and the text can follow the lines of the image itself.

Other features

Other useful features found in most desktop publishing packages include:

- the ability to work in layers (see page 84)
- colour handling facilities necessary for printing from a printing press
- comprehensive master pages
- HTML export for Web page creation
- spelling, hyphenation and widow/orphan controls
- automated numbering, indexing and contents.

Databases

A database is a collection of related data items, which are linked and structured so that the data can be accessed in a number of ways.

A simple database consists of only one set of data. This is called a flat file. An example of a flat file database is PinPoint or Microsoft® Works.

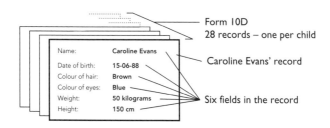

A doctors' surgery may use a database to store information about patients including their medical history, any current treatments, dates of inoculations, etc (see page 114).

A relational database is more complex (see page 96). Relational databases are very powerful as they allow the data to be accessed in many different ways. An example of a relational database is Microsoft® Access.

On larger commercial systems, there will be many users accessing the data at the same time. Examples of these relational databases include Oracle and Microsoft® SQL Server.

Functions of a database

A database program on a computer is designed to hold information (data). Often the amount of information stored is very large and it would take a long time for us to search through this information if it were written on paper. Holding the information in a database enables us to search very quickly and to sort the information easily. The required data can then be printed out as a report.

An example database

Suppose you wished to create a books database. You could ask each pupil in the class to bring in details of ten books from home. These details could then be added to the class database. Using this database, you could examine the selection of books to determine the:

- most popular publisher
- most popular author
- average number of pages
- average number of chapters
- average number of pages per chapter
- average cost of the books
- most/least popular books.

Typical information for a book might include:

> *The Worst Witch All At Sea* is written by Jill Murphy and published by Penguin. Its ISBN is 0 670 83253 7. It costs £8.99, has 21 chapters and 222 pages. I thought it was excellent and gave it a rating of 9 out of 10.

In the computer database each book would make up a record. Within the record, the details of the book are structured into fields (see page 91).

Title	The Worst Witch All At Sea		
Author	Jill Murphy		
Price	£8.99	Publisher	Penguin
Pages	222	ISBN	0 670 83253 7
Chapters	21	Rating/10	9
Comment	Excellent		

Structuring the data in this way enables the database program to search, sort, display and print the data easily. With the data now contained in specific fields, if you wished to search for the book with the most pages, you would instigate a search of the 'Pages' field in each record throughout the database. Structuring the data also enables you to see if a field is empty and whether or not important information is missing.

Sorting

Being able to sort the data is an important function of a database package. The steps involved in sorting data are listed below:

Example

1   Select the field you wish to use to sort by; this might be a 'Surname' field or 'Account number' field. Sometimes you may wish to choose a secondary field to sort by. For example, if the main sort is by surname, a secondary sort would be by first name in case there were several people with the same surname.

2   Decide whether the list should be in ascending ('A' at the top and 'Z' at the bottom) or descending order.

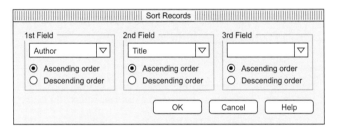

Here the instructions given to the database are to do a main sort by author and a secondary sort by the title of the book

Record	Author	Title	Publisher	Price
37	Montgomery L M	Anne of Avonlea	Puffin	£2.99
53	Montgomery R	Chinese Dragon	Bantam	£2.99
46	Montgomery R	War With The Evil Monster	Bantam	£1.25
94	Murphy J	The Worst Witch All At Sea	Penguin	£8.99
21	Oliver M	Agent Arthur on the Stormy Seas	Usborne	£2.75
34	Oliver M	Agent Arthur's Arctic Adventure	Usborne	£2.50
75	Oliver M	Agent Arthur's Jungle Journey	Usborne	£2.75
38	Pearce C	Something Really Wild	Lions	£12.99
54	Pratchett T	Only You Can Save Mankind	Transworld	£3.99

125K used   record 19 of 105

The data is now sorted by author and then title

Note: When you do a sort, numbers come before letters and, depending on the database software, lowercase letters come before uppercase letters.

Searching

To be able to retrieve information from a database, particularly from a large database, is vitally important. This is done by the computer taking the user's request and searching for a match in the database. The steps necessary to carry out a search are:

1 Choose the 'query' or 'find' option.

2 Specify which field in the record you wish to search.

3 Decide the condition statement:

'is equal to'	'is greater than'
'is not equal to'	'is less than or equal to'
'is greater than or equal to'	'contains'.

4 Enter the value to be searched for.

5 If another condition needs to be applied to the search, go back to step 2; otherwise start the search.

Example

1 To search the books database to find a book with 'witches' and 'wizards' in the title, you might use the following search:

Title 'contains' "Witch"   OR   Title 'contains' "Wizard"

Note: The use of the condition 'contains' will find the word as part of the title and will also find "Witches" and "Wizards".

2 To search for a highly rated (rating of 10) and cheap book (£5 or less) you might use the search:

Rating 'is equal to' 10   AND   Price 'is less than or equal to' 5

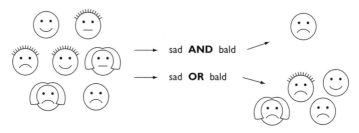

How the AND and OR criteria work

The words AND and OR used between different search statements are called Boolean operators.

Database forms

When you are entering data into a database, you can design the layout by placing boxes and labels on to the screen where the data is to be typed into the different fields. These data input screens are often referred to as forms.

Database reports

Database reports can be designed by the user to show the data or, more usually, print out data from the database. When creating a report, the user can choose whether all or just some of the fields in the database record are to be printed. Data can be printed in columns and numeric fields can be totalled at the bottom of each page and at the end of the report.

Database fields

Each record of a database contains fields where the data or information is stored. When a new database is being designed, many database packages request the user to specify the type of data that will be entered into each of the fields. This allows the computer to process the data effectively and allocate computer memory efficiently.

Different types of field include:

- **Text field** – Letters or numbers, eg 'Car registration' = W741GEV.
- **Number field** – Numbers which can be used for statistics or calculations. Number fields can be divided further into 'integer' fields (numbers without decimal places) and 'real' numbers (with decimal places). For example, 'Age' = 15 or 'Price' = 12.95.
- **Date/time field** – These fields are specifically designed to store dates and times which can then be displayed in different formats, eg 2 April 1952 might be displayed in the form:

d-mmmm-yyyy	= 2 April 1952
dd-mmm-yy	= 02-Apr-52
dd-mm-yy	= 02-04-52

  Holding dates in a date field allows searches to take place, eg show records where 'Last payment date' is greater than 1 November 2000.
- **Boolean or logical field** – In these fields only a 'Yes' or 'No' value will be accepted or a 'True' or 'False' value. For example, 'Has the membership been paid?'.

- **Memo field** – This is similar to a text field in that it can hold letters and numbers. Memo fields are used when larger amounts of data are entered into the field. 64 000 characters are allowed in Microsoft® Access, whereas the maximum number of characters allowed in a text field is 255.

- **Calculation field** – This is used when the field displays a calculation based on numbers in other fields. For example, 'Area of circle' = 3.142 x ('Radius field')^2.

- **Picture/image field** – Many modern databases now have a field where pictures can be displayed within the record. The data entered into this field by the user would include file details of the image to be displayed.

Coding information

It is sometimes useful to code information in database fields. Say, for example, pupils were entering the subjects studied at school, they might code these as:

MA = Maths	EN = English
FR = French	DT = Design and Technology

Advantages:

- easier and quicker to enter
- less typing required
- less likely to make spelling mistakes
- uses less computer memory
- allows fixed length fields.

Fixed length records

When a database has fixed length records, then each field within the record is allocated a fixed number of bytes.

Advantages:

- It is easier for the computer to process because if you edit a field and save the record back to the disk, it will take up exactly the same space as before.

- It makes locating a particular record very rapid as the position for the start of each record is known.

Disadvantage:

- If data is too long to fit into a field, it must be abbreviated and if it is shorter that the space allocated then memory is being wasted.

Fixed length records

Variable length records

= end of field marker

How data is stored for fixed and variable length records

Variable length records

Here the fields in a record can vary in size and even the number of fields can vary. As the field and record size is not set, special characters (end of field markers and end of record markers) must be inserted to show the ends.

Advantages:

- Useful where databases hold mainly text.
- Memory is not wasted by empty spaces.

Disadvantages:

- More difficult for the computer to process.
- Lengthening a field entry while editing may mean the record cannot be saved back onto the disk in the original position.

Key fields

The key field is the one used to identify each record and is often used when searching and sorting the records. If the record contains a field like an account number and this is a unique number only for that record, then this field is called the primary key field. If there is not a unique primary key, the key field can be formed from several fields, eg 'First address line' and 'Postcode'. This is called a composite key.

Information and data

The two words 'information' and 'data' often seem to mean the same thing. We put information into computers which is stored as data. There is, however, a subtle difference between the two. If, for example, the data in a computer was '02041952', what would this mean? Is it a part number? An account number? A telephone number? If you know it is a date, then we understand it means 2 April 1952.

Information = Data + 'The context and structure of the data'

Data capture

If we are going to search and sort data in a database then it is necessary to capture the data first. This can be done using any of the input devices mentioned earlier, although some are more commonly used than others. Using a questionnaire to gather data and entering this via the keyboard is still one of the most common methods.

Validation

Validation is the name given to the checks a computer can carry out when data is input. Whatever form of input device is used, some form of check can be made on the data entering the computer.

Example: A database field in a secondary school timetable package contains information about the teacher, subject and year group. This information is coded as follows:

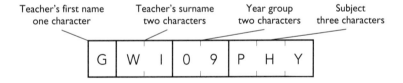

This shows the code entered for Mr G Williams teaching Physics to Year 9. Here are some checks to make sure that the data has been entered correctly:

- **Presence check** – The field cannot be left empty when completing the record.
- **Character count** – There should always be eight characters in this field; more or fewer would prompt the user to edit the data.

- **Range check** – The fourth and fifth characters are extracted from the code and converted to a number. The validation check then ensures that the number is 'equal to or greater than' 7 AND 'less than or equal to' 13 (assuming the school has a sixth form).
- **Table (or File) lookup** – Here the teacher's code (first three characters) and the subject code (last three characters) can be checked by opening a separate table and ensuring the codes do exist in a valid list.
- **Picture check** – This checks that the data entered in this field is as expected, ie TTTNNTTT (where T = text and N = number).

There are also a number of totalling checks that can be carried out when processing data. Take, for example, a payroll program which is run at the end of each month to calculate wages. The hours worked by each employee are input to disk in preparation for running the payroll program.

At the front of the data, in a batch header record, several extra pieces of information can be included. These enable the computer program to check the data being entered and report any errors. This data includes:

- **Batch totals** – how many records are being processed.
- **Control totals** – a manually calculated figure, eg the total hours worked.
- **Hash totals** – a total, often quite meaningless, figure calculated by the computer, eg the sum of all the employee numbers.

These checks help to ensure that the program processes the payroll accurately and that no employees are left out or are paid incorrectly.

Check digits

Some numbers are given an extra digit on the end which is called a check digit. This digit is calculated from the original number and acts as a check when the number is read by the computer. There are several ways in which these check digits are calculated. One popular method is called the modulus-11 method.

When the computer reads the number (including the check digit), it checks the calculation and gives an error message if it is not correct. This procedure traps 99% of common errors like getting two digits mixed up.

Numbers that use check digits include customer account numbers, International Standard Book Numbers (ISBNs) and the numbers on bar codes. You may have noticed at the checkout till of the supermarket that some products have to be passed several times across the scanner before the beep tells the assistant it has been read correctly. Each time a product is scanned, the number associated with the black and white lines is validated using the check digit.

Relational databases

The type of database introduced earlier in this section is called a flat file database. The data is held in a single file and the sorting, searching and printing of reports is done on this datafile. This type of database is suitable for use at home or in school but it would not be adequate for larger businesses and organisations. Here a large amount of data is required and it is necessary to separate the data into tables with each table holding data relating to one subject or entity.

In relational databases, the tables of data exist independently from the programs which may use them. The database management system (DBMS) provides the software tools to link the tables together and do searches of the data. Each user may have a different view of the database, with restricted data only being accessible to those with the necessary authority. Different departments and individuals can be given permission to edit and update parts of the data. For example, the sales department may be given the task of ensuring the customer data is kept up-to-date.

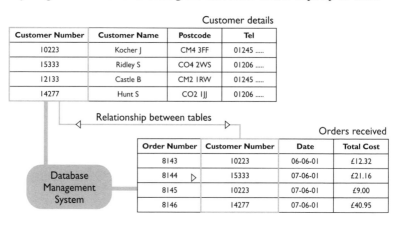

Customer details

Customer Number	Customer Name	Postcode	Tel
10223	Kocher J	CM4 3FF	01245 .....
15333	Ridley S	CO4 2WS	01206 .....
12133	Castle B	CM2 1RW	01245 .....
14277	Hunt S	CO2 1JJ	01206 .....

Relationship between tables

Orders received

Order Number	Customer Number	Date	Total Cost
8143	10223	06-06-01	£12.32
8144	15333	07-06-01	£21.16
8145	10223	07-06-01	£9.00
8146	14277	07-06-01	£40.95

Database Management System

In relational databases, data is grouped into tables

Spreadsheets

A spreadsheet is a computer program which is designed to display and process numbers. It is made up of a grid into which numbers are entered. The program contains many mathematical, statistical and financial calculations which can be applied to the numbers. Many spreadsheets can also show the numbers in the form of graphs.

A spreadsheet is a very useful and powerful tool for experimenting with numbers and asking 'What if ...?' (see page 100).

The illustration below shows a screen from a typical spreadsheet program. Each column of cells has a letter at the top and each row has a number on the left. By using the letter for the column and the number for the row, we can address each cell individually. We can move from one cell to another by entering the new cell address, using the arrow keys on the keyboard or by pointing and clicking with the mouse.

Editing bar

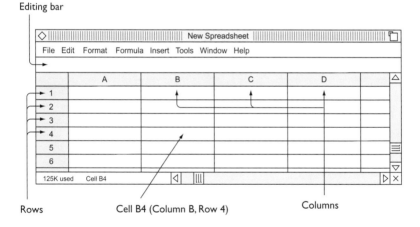

Rows   Cell B4 (Column B, Row 4)   Columns

Spreadsheet cells

Cells in the spreadsheet may contain numbers, text (letters, words, etc), dates and formulas. Each cell, or a block of cells, may be 'formatted' so that the contents of the cell is displayed in different ways.

The way a number appears in the cell is controlled through formatting the cell. For example, to display £12.50, then:

- enter 12.5

- highlight the cell (or the row or column)

- format the cell to display currency with two decimal places.

Number
24.3 is entered and then formatted £###0.00.
The cell then displays £24.30

Date
5.2.97 is entered and then formatted as dd-mmm-yyyy.
Displayed as 05-Sep-2001

	A	B	C	D	
1	£24.30		37		
2		6			
3				05-Sep-2001	
4					
5	37			24	
6					

New Spreadsheet

File Edit Format Formula Insert Tools Window Help

125K used   Cell B4

Cell reference
Reference = C1, therefore cell A5 displays the same as cell C1, ie 37

Calculation
Calculation entered = B2*4.
Cell B2 contains 6;
6 x 4 = 24;
therefore the cell displays 24

When a cell is selected, the contents of the cell are shown on the editing bar but the result of any calculation is displayed in the cell.

The illustration below shows some of the different ways numbers can be formatted in the cells of a spreadsheet. This example shows how the number 12345.6789 would be displayed in the various formats:

Format	Example*	Description
0	12346	integer
0.00	12345.68	2 decimal places
#,##0	12,346	integer with thousands separator
£0.00	£12345.68	pounds and pence
0%	1234568%	integer percentage
0.00E+00	1.23E+04	3 significant figures plus exponent

Calculations

The power of a spreadsheet comes from its ability to do calculations with numbers. The contents of one cell can be calculated from other cells in the sheet.

Formula = A2*B2.

Sometimes when students see this kind of spreadsheet they want to type the answer '12' straight into cell C2. Cell C2 should contain A2*B2. If the number in cell A2 or B2 is now changed, the new area will automatically be calculated in cell C2.

Formulae and functions

Spreadsheet packages come with a library of formulae and functions as part of the program. There are formulae for financial calculations, for handling dates and times, for mathematical and statistical work and for logical expressions. In the example on the next page, two of the many functions are illustrated – the SUM and the IF function.

An example of using a function to show the results of an examination is given below. The pass mark is 40% and the formulae in the right-hand column shows whether the student has passed or failed:

	A	B	C	D	E	D	E
1			Paper 1	Paper 2	Paper 3	Total	PASS/
2			(30%)	(30%)	(40%)	(%)	FAIL
3	Katie-Marie	NORMAN	12	14	20	=SUM(C3:E3)	=IF(F3>39,"PASS", "FAIL")
4	Noel	LUFF	4	5	15	=SUM(C4:E4)	=IF(F4>39,"PASS", "FAIL")
5	Catherine	OAKLEY	15	19	27	=SUM(C5:E5)	=IF(F5>39,"PASS", "FAIL")
6	Laura	ODD	9	13	30	=SUM(C6:E6)	=IF(F6>39,"PASS", "FAIL")
7	Matthew	LAWRIE	13	9	17	=SUM(C7:E7)	=IF(F7>39,"PASS", "FAIL")

The IF function

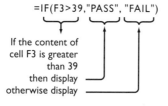

=IF(F3>39,"PASS", "FAIL")

If the content of
cell F3 is greater
than 39
then display ———
otherwise display ———

The SUM function

=SUM(C3:E3)

Add up the content
of cells C3 to E3
(ie C3+D3+E3)

	A	B	C	D	E	D	E
1			Paper 1	Paper 2	Paper 3	Total	PASS/
2			(30%)	(30%)	(40%)	(%)	FAIL
3	Katie-Marie	NORMAN	12	14	20	46	PASS
4	Noel	LUFF	4	5	15	24	FAIL
5	Catherine	OAKLEY	15	19	27	61	PASS
6	Laura	ODD	9	13	30	52	PASS
7	Matthew	LAWRIE	13	9	17	39	FAIL

'What if...?'

'What if...?' is a phrase often associated with spreadsheets. If a number in one cell is changed then the value in another cell may also change since it uses the first number in a calculation. The second cell may change a third cell, and so on through the sheet. The values in your spreadsheet model can be recalculated instantly when you change the contents of individual cells, for example, "What if the price is increased to ...?", "What if the sales fall by ...?", "What if the VAT rate changes to ...?", etc.

Constructing a spreadsheet

The sheet below shows the sales from the school tuck shop for a week:

	A	B	C	D	E	F
1		Crisps	Mars bars	Snickers	Apples	
2	Mon	17	22	12	11	
3	Tue	23	19	7	14	
4	Wed	24	16	8	9	
5	Thu	18	17	9	11	
6	Fri	21	16	13	12	
7	Total sold					
8						
9	Sale price	25	30	25	20	
10	Cost price	20	24	18	10	
11						
12	Total sales					
13	Total costs					
14						
15	Weekly profit					

1 In column F, we can total the number of items sold each day. In cell F2, we would use the formula =sum(B2:E2). After entering this, the cell F2 would display the answer 62. To insert this calculation for Tuesday to Friday in cells F3 to F6, we copy or replicate the calculation in F2.

2 In row 7, we can total the individual items sold during the week. In cell B7, we would enter the formula =sum(B2:B6). We would then copy this formula into cells C7 to E7.

3 To find how much money or income we have made from the sales of each item, we need to add a formula to the cells in row 12. In B12, the formula is =B7*B9; this will work out how much money we have made during the week from the sale of crisps.

4 The items sold at the tuck shop need to be purchased by the school. Row 10 of the sheet shows the cost for each item. In row 13, we need to show the total costs for the items sold during the week. The formula for this is =B7*B10.

	A	B	C	D	E	F
1		Crisps	Mars bars	Snickers	Apples	
2	Mon	17	22	12	11	62
3	Tue	23	19	7	14	63
4	Wed	24	16	8	9	57
5	Thu	18	17	9	11	55
6	Fri	21	16	13	12	62
7	Total sold	103	90	49	57	
8						
9	Sale price	25	30	25	20	
10	Cost price	20	24	18	10	
11						
12	Total sales	2575	2700	1225	1140	
13	Total costs	2060	2160	882	570	
14						
15	Weekly profit	515	540	343	570	

5　The profit is the difference between the selling price and the buying price. Therefore the formula needed for row 15 is
= B12-B13.

6　Our final task is to copy the formulas in B12, B13 and B15 across the sheet.

Note: All of the money values in the sheet are shown in pence. It would be easier to show the larger numbers in rows 12, 13 and 15 in pounds. This can be done in two steps:

7　Divide by 100 to change pence into pounds.

8　Format the cells to currency to show the £ sign.

	A	B	C	D	E	F
12	Total sales	£25.75	£27.00	£12.25	£11.40	
13	Total costs	£20.60	£21.60	£8.82	£5.70	
14						
15	Weekly profit	£5.15	£5.40	£3.43	£5.70	

Payroll program

Since the early days of computing, the payroll program has been used to calculate the salaries and wages for employees. It is an ideal example of 'batch' processing where all the data is collected first and then the payroll program is set to run with little, or minimal further input from the operator. The data for manual work consists of the hours worked, still determined in some companies by employees clocking in and out. The payroll program calculates the salaries and wages, the overtime payments, sick pay, holiday pay, income tax, National insurance contributions and pensions. The hourly rates and gross salaries are held on file and accessed as the program works through each employee's salaries. The monthly data is added to a master file for each employee which holds the accumulated totals of the figures for the current tax year. The payslips are printed as part of the payroll operation.

The majority of organisations now pay the salaries and wages directly into the employee's bank account. As part of the computer payroll run, a file is prepared holding a list of the staff, their bank account details and the salary payments. This data is transmitted electronically to BACS (Bankers' Automated Clearing Service) where it is processed and the money transferred between the banks. This payment processes takes three days to complete.

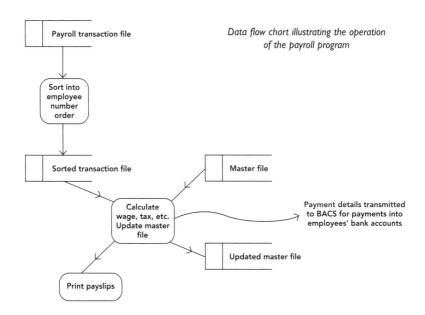

Data flow chart illustrating the operation of the payroll program

Presentation graphics

A presentation graphics program allows the user to prepare and give a presentation onscreen for an audience to view. Usually the presentation is assembled as a collection of slides. Each slide may contain text, clip art, graphics, drawings, video, sound or animation. By working alongside the screen presentation, the user has total control over how the slides are presented. Alternatively, the presentation can be left unattended to cycle through automatically and then loop back to the beginning.

A popular presentation graphics program is Microsoft® PowerPoint. Many home users, schools and businesses use Microsoft® Office on their computers. PowerPoint is one of the programs incorporated in the Office collection along with Microsoft® Word and Excel. Teachers find presentation graphics programs such as PowerPoint particularly useful in the classroom to deliver material. Students find the package enjoyable to use as the slides are quick to generate and it gives a professional feel to their work.

Preparing the slides

When starting a new slide show, the first choice will be to decide on the background to the slides. The package provides a selection of prepared slide background designs to choose from or the user can design their own. The illustration on the right shows a design that makes the slide look like a notebook.

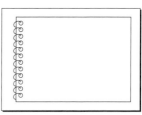

The next decision involves the content and layout of the slide. Again, the presentation program offers ready-made suggestions but the more experienced user can start with a blank slide and create their own design. The illustration shows some of the layouts offered by the program.

By clicking on each area of the slide, the title, text and graphics can be inserted. The illustration shows a completed slide for some information about Paris.

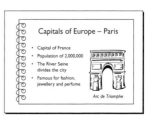

Often, the presentation package will provide complete sets of slides ready for the user to insert their specific details. Slide sets have the advantage of prompting the user for detail and helping them to design a coherent presentation.

Microsoft® PowerPoint, for example, provides ready-made slide sets for:

- business plans
- company meetings
- advertising fliers
- marketing meetings
- organisation structures
- sales presentations.

Animation

Animation of the slides in the presentation can help to make more of an impact with the audience. The change from one slide to the next can be animated in over 40 different ways. For example, the new slide can appear like a Venetian blind opening or by wiping across the old slide from the sides or bottom. Sounds can accompany these slide changes and the program offers a range of sounds to choose from.

Once a slide is onscreen, the text and graphics can be made to appear through animation. They can 'drive' in, 'fly' onto the slide or appear with a camera-shutter effect. Individual letters on the slide can be projected onto the slide by a laser or a typewriter or by dropping down from the top of the slide.

Output

The presentation through a series of slides has been discussed but other outputs are available. These include:

- slides with speaker's handouts and notes
- overhead projection slides
- 35 mm slides
- video conferencing
- files for transmission across a network.

Multimedia

For teaching and learning

Multimedia offers both the student and the teacher a valuable resource for teaching and learning. Multimedia packages consist of text, graphics, sound, animations, photographs, full motion video, hyperlinks, Internet links, questions, puzzles and quizzes. The key feature of a multimedia package is its interactivity with the user; students can explore by choosing their own route through the package, learning at their own speed.

Another important feature is the wealth of resource material which students can transfer across into their project work by copying the material to the computer's clipboard and then pasting it into their own document. Many multimedia packages contain extensive collections of photographs that can be particularly useful for school projects.

Why are multimedia packages on CD/DVDs?

The graphics, audio and video clips contained in multimedia packages use up a lot of memory so it is not possible to distribute programs on floppy disk. CD-ROMs, which can store up to 650 MB of data, are the most common medium for holding multimedia packages, although this amount of storage is insufficient for some titles.

One of the versions of the popular encyclopedia Microsoft® Encarta Reference Suite 2001 is now available on one DVD, the equivalent version on CD-ROM requires three discs which need to be swapped in and out of the CD-drive as the program is used.

Topics available

There are now multimedia packages, often written by experienced teachers, covering topics in every subject of the school curriculum. These programs often illustrate processes that would be difficult to show using traditional teaching methods and allow students to learn at their own pace in an interactive way.

Some reference packages are useful across all subject boundaries. For example, a selection of encyclopedias are available including Compton's, Hutchinson, Oxford, Kingfisher, Encarta and Britannica.

Web browsers

The Web browser makes the Internet accessible and useful to the ordinary user. It is software which interprets HyperText Markup Language (HTML) code, and displays the result in a window. This is a system of 'tags' which are embedded in the text of the pages to control how it is displayed, the placing of graphics and how hypertext links work.

Although there are many browsers available, the two most widely used are Microsoft® Internet Explorer and Netscape Navigator. These programs are widely available (free) and one of them is likely to be provided with your ISP start-up package.

All browsers have a few essential common features including:

- a scrollable window which allows you to move up and down pages
- **Back** and **Forward** buttons which allow you to move backwards and forwards through the sequence of pages you have seen in your current session (this will usually happen without reloading the pages from the remote computer because your browser stores – or caches – them in memory and/or on disk)
- a **Home** button to take you back to your default home page
- a **Search** button for access to the major search engines

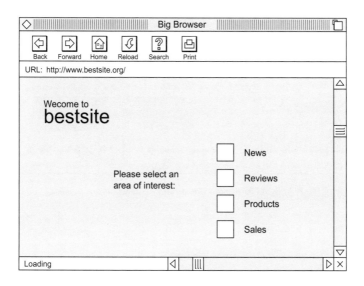

- somewhere to type in the URL (the Internet address, which normally starts with http:// for Web pages) of any page you want to see
- a bookmark facility, sometimes called favourites, which allows you to find useful pages again quickly and efficiently
- the ability to print pages
- a method of saving any information you find.

If you can use these basic facilities, you will be able to find, copy and use information from anywhere on the Internet.

Plug-ins

A plug-in is an add-on piece of software for your browser. Just as most Web pages have images on them as well as text, some pages have special objects on them which require a plug-in to be viewed correctly. Most browsers will now detect if a page requires a plug-in that you do not have and direct you to a download page from where you can acquire the plug-in. Usually, this involves downloading an installer program which you then run to install the plug-in.

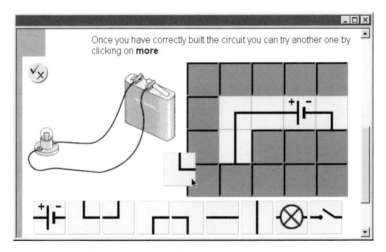

Plug-ins add functionality like the ability to create interactive tools

System design and development

When we set out to use Information and Communication Technology to assist with a particular task, we follow a structured series of processes. The stages in this series are similar whether carried out by a team of programmers for a company or a student doing a coursework project for their ICT GCSE. The general pattern for the stages is as follows:

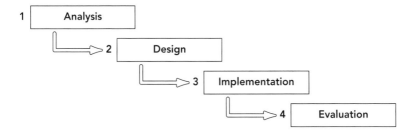

These two additional parts must also be included, either as separate stages, or as part of the ones above:

Feasibility study

After a detailed examination of the problem and research, it is necessary to look at whether a computerised solution is the right approach. Will the computerised solution being proposed reduce paperwork, speed up the processing, give better stock control, create fewer mistakes, provide better reports for the managers? Will these potential benefits outweigh the costs involved of introducing the new system? Will it be beneficial to use a computer system rather than people to carry out the tasks? It should be clear that the answer to this question is 'Yes' before a decision to proceed is reached.

Top-down design

There are several methods of designing a solution for a chosen problem but one of the most popular methods is using a 'top-down design' approach. Starting with the main task, this is broken down into sub-tasks. These sub-tasks are then further divided to show more detail.

An example of a top-down approach is shown in the illustration below. Here a computer program is being designed for teachers that will enable them to write reports for students:

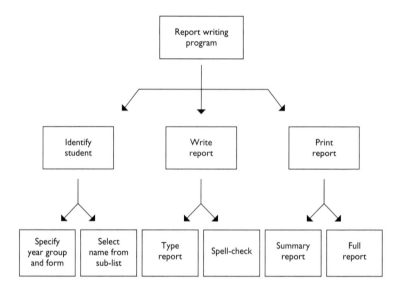

The bottom layer would then be subdivided further until the whole task comprised a set of simple tasks.

Testing

Testing is a very important part in the development of an ICT system. A plan for testing and the results of testing should also be documented to show that it has been carried out in a logical fashion.

Documentation

There are two types of documentation – user documentation and technical documentation:

- **User documentation** – The user documentation is designed for the person using the new system and should include:
    - how to load and run the program
    - how to use the different features of the program such as entering data, saving, editing, sorting and printing
    - a troubleshooting section to deal with exceptional circumstances where things do not work as they should.

    User documentation should be written in plain English without any technical words or terms.

- **Technical documentation** – This documentation contains the technical details of the program together with structure diagrams to assist other programmers and systems analysts. It is, therefore, written using technical words and terms. Technical documentation allows changes to be made to the program in future years when the original developers may no longer be around. Programs may need to be improved or updated. For example, many programs were altered to cater for the date change in the year 2000.

Data protection

The Data Protection Act (1998)

The 'right to privacy' is a right we all expect. We do not expect personal details such as our age, medical records, personal family details, political and religious beliefs to be freely available to everybody. With the growth of Information and Communication Technology, large databases are able to hold huge quantities of information and global networks are able to share and distribute this information around the world in seconds. In order to control this development and to protect people's right to privacy, the Data Protection Act was introduced. The first Act became law in 1984 but was replaced by the 1998 Act that also incorporates the European Commission Directive.

If any person, organisation, company or business wishes to hold personal information about people, they must register with the Office of the Data Protection Commissioner.

The Data Protection Act contains eight basic principles. A summary of these is shown below:

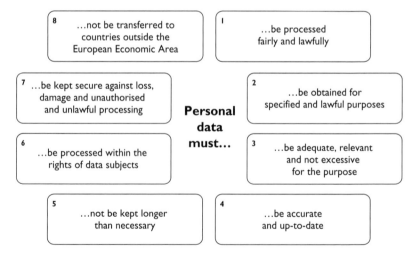

8 ...not be transferred to countries outside the European Economic Area

1 ...be processed fairly and lawfully

7 ...be kept secure against loss, damage and unauthorised and unlawful processing

Personal data must...

2 ...be obtained for specified and lawful purposes

6 ...be processed within the rights of data subjects

3 ...be adequate, relevant and not excessive for the purpose

5 ...not be kept longer than necessary

4 ...be accurate and up-to-date

Note: The first of the eight principles listed above contains the most details in the Act as different conditions apply according to the nature of the data held. Also, unlike the 1984 Act, manual records containing data are now subject to legislation.

Personal data

What is actually meant by personal data? It must relate to living people who can be identified, and is data that expresses an opinion about a person or the intentions of the data-holders towards that person. The data can be further classified as 'sensitive' personal data. This includes details of:

- racial or ethnic origins
- political opinions
- religious beliefs
- whether members of Trade Unions
- their physical or mental health or condition
- sexual life.

Rights of data subjects

In the sixth of the eight principles shown, the rights of the individal were mentioned. The rights of individuals have increased substantially in the 1998 Act. The following offers a summary.

The individual can:

- be given a copy of the data held
- prevent processing of the data if it is likely to cause damage or distress
- prevent the data being used for direct marketing
- prevent automated decisions being made on the basis of data held
- receive compensation for damage and distress caused by use of the data
- have data corrected, blocked and erased if inaccurate
- make a request to the Data Protection Commissioner if they feel the Act has been contravened.

Exemptions

There are certain exemptions to the Act and the rules governing the need to register data. A summary of the main exemptions to the Act include data that is:

- related to national security
- associated with crime and taxation
- involved in health, education and social work
- used in regulatory activities by public 'watch dogs'

- processed for special (journalism, literary and artistic) purposes
- used in research, history and statistics
- required by law and in connection with legal proceedings being disclosed
- held for domestic purposes, eg household, personal and family affairs.

Who stores what?

Many organisations store personal data. In most cases, the data will include your name, address and telephone number. The following list suggests some of the additional data that may be stored by some organisations:

- **School** – marital status, emergency contact details (eg mobile phone number), previous school(s) attended, examination results, attendance records.
- **Doctor** – medical history, any allergies, details of repeat prescriptions, date and type of inoculations, current treatments, results of tests.
- **Bank** – details of payments made from account and deposits, standing orders and direct debits, loan details, overdraft limit, details of when and where you used your cards.
- **Supermarket** – how much you have spent, what you bought, the dates and times you visited the supermarket.

Looking after computer data

In business, the data stored in a computer can be hundreds of times more valuable than the actual computer equipment. This data may include all the company's financial records, all its customers' details, records of the stock held, etc. Losing this data could, in some cases, put companies out of business.

Data can be damaged or destroyed in the following ways:

- breakdown of hardware, particularly disk drives
- mistakes by office staff, eg deleting files
- poor office practice, eg not taking a regular back-up of data files and not checking for viruses
- hackers gaining access to systems and changing/deleting data
- computer fraud where data is changed to benefit individuals

- theft of computer equipment
- fire, floods, hurricanes, earthquakes, etc, destroying equipment
- infection of systems and data by computer viruses
- deliberate and malicious damage by staff.

Back-ups

Taking a back-up of the data from the hard disk drive of a computer or from the hard disk of a server running a network is vital. One certain fact is that a hard disk drive will not run forever. If a back-up is taken at the end of each day, then the most that can be lost is one day's work. Often special tape streamer units are used which save the data onto magnetic tape cassettes. These cassette tapes can typically hold up to 26 GB of data, allowing all the data on the server's hard drives to be backed up. A number of tapes should be used in rotation so that a back-up copy can always be kept away from the premises.

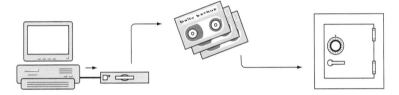

Data is backed up onto tape and then put in a safe place

Businesses may encourage office staff to take back-up tapes home with them so that data will not be lost through theft from the offices. Tapes kept on-site should be deposited safely each evening in a fireproof safe. Remember, in the event of a power cut, work that has not been saved may be lost. Save your work regularly as back-up files only hold data from previous days.

Hackers

A hacker is a person who breaks codes and passwords to gain unauthorised entry to computer systems. Hackers can do an enormous amount of damage if they break into a computer system. For some people, the challenge of breaking the codes is irresistible and so precautions have to be taken. Stand-alone computers are usually safe as there is no connection for the hackers to break into. Computers which form part of networks or those with external links, such as attached modems, are in danger from hackers. It is necessary to use passwords to log on to the computer system and it is important to change these passwords at regular intervals.

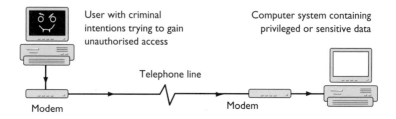

User with criminal intentions trying to gain unauthorised access

Computer system containing privileged or sensitive data

Telephone line

Modem

Modem

Computers connected to networks or modems are at risk from hacking

Computer fraud

Computer fraud is a criminal activity where computer operators use the computer to their own advantage. It is thought that only one in ten cases of computer fraud are reported. There are a number of reasons for this:

- It is very hard to track down and the people committing the crime are often very clever.
- Offenders are often young, with no previous criminal records.
- When fraud is discovered in a company, it is often not publicised as news of the fraud may damage the image of the company.

One example of computer fraud involved a computer operator who found a blank payroll form. He completed the form, making up the details for an imaginary person working in the company. Each month, as the pay cheques were produced from the company computer, he was able to slip the cheque into his pocket without anyone realising.

Computer viruses

In the same way that human viruses use the human body's own system to reproduce themselves, so computer viruses are small programs that 'hijack' a computer and use it to reproduce and spread themselves.

How viruses spread

There are hundreds of different viruses and more are being created every month by people intent on damaging other people's computer systems. The viruses attach themselves to computer programs and data files. They then spread by copying themselves onto floppy disks, then onto other hard disks and also across networks – all without the knowledge of the user. It is quite possible to connect to the Internet, download an email message and gain a virus in the process.

How they are activated

Viruses are activated in different ways. Some are activated by the internal clock and will start running on a particular day, eg Friday 13. Others activate when a series of conditions are true, eg when a certain combination of keys are pressed on the keyboard. Most virus programs are harmless, but some can destroy and corrupt data on the computer's hard disk.

Removing viruses

There are a number of anti-virus programs available for wiping out viruses but, with any anti-virus program, it is important to have regular updates to deal with new viruses. When the anti-virus software is run, it scans the hard disk looking for virus patterns. This software cleans the virus off the disk and alerts the user to the damage caused by the virus.

Trojan horse

A Trojan horse is a destructive program that pretends to be a useful application. Unlike viruses, Trojan horses do not replicate themselves but they can be just as destructive. One of the most insidious types of Trojan horse is a program that claims to rid your computer of viruses but instead introduces them to your computer!

The Computer Misuse Act, 1990

Hacking, computer fraud and computer viruses are all relatively new crimes that established English laws were not designed to deal with. For example, under existing laws a hacker could only be prosecuted for the theft of electricity. To deal with these new crimes, a law was introduced in 1990 called The Computer Misuse Act. Under this law, the following offences could be dealt with:

- **Hacking** – Unauthorised access to any program or data held in a computer. Penalty is a maximum fine of £2000 and a six-month prison sentence.
- **Computer fraud and blackmail** – Penalty is an unlimited fine and a maximum five-year prison sentence.

- **Viruses** – Unauthorised modification of the contents of a computer, impairing the operation of any program or reliability of data. Penalty is an unlimited fine and a maximum five-year prison sentence.

The Copyright, Designs and Patents Act, 1989

Copying computer software, or software piracy, is now a criminal offence under this 1989 Act. The Act covers stealing software, using illegally copied software and manuals, and running purchased software on two or more machines at the same time without a suitable licence. Quite often, organisations will purchase software licences to cover the number of workstations on their network. They then neglect to purchase additional software licences as they buy more workstations.

The legal penalties for breaking the copyright law include unlimited fines and up to two years in prison.

It has been estimated that half the software used is copied illegally and in some countries pirated software accounts for 90% of the total. Two organisations fight to stop software being copied:

- FAST (Federation Against Software Theft), founded in 1984, is a non-profit organisation to promote the legal use of software.
- BSA (Business Software Alliance) exist to make organisations and their employees aware of the law and encourage its implementation.

Various types of licence exist for software. These include:

- **Single-user licence** where software can only be used on one computer. This is the most usual form of licence.
- **Multi-user licence** where an organisation may install the software on an agreed number of computers.
- **Site licence** where any number of computers may use the software at a single location.
- **Freeware** has a licence allowing free use and distribution of the software. In the UK, freeware is often called 'public domain software'.
- **Shareware** has a licence allowing free use of the software for a trial period. If the user wishes to continue using the software, they must pay a fee. This often entitles them to support, manuals and improved versions.

Health and safety

Most health and safety rulings apply only to users who are at the computer for an hour or more at a time. Hence, this should not be a problem in school. However, following the general principles of the health and safety rulings still remains important, both as general good practice and to instil good habits into students.

Safe working conditions

Unlike many other items of equipment, computers do not have dangerous moving parts which threaten the user. They are, nevertheless, electrical devices attached to a 240V power supply and should be treated carefully.

All cables should be safely out of the way where they can neither be accidentally dislodged or form a hazard to people passing. The computer should be properly earthed and the plugs should have the correct fuses. A surge protector will guard against spikes in the power supply. If the computer is being moved or opened, then ensure that the power cables are the first to be disconnected and the last to be reconnected.

Conducting liquids (including water, tea, coffee, soft drinks, etc) should not be allowed near the machines. There should be adequate and appropriate fire safety equipment available. Fire extinguishers should be powder- or CO_2-based, not water-based.

You need to create comfortable working conditions to prevent fatigue and strains. Many people find that extended periods of looking at a computer screen give them eye strain or headaches, and repetitive strain injuries involving wrists, elbows, forearms and necks are common in people who regularly use computers for long periods of time. These can generally be avoided by sensible arrangement of the parts of the computer and an appropriate screen setup.

The keyboard and mouse should be placed where they can be easily and comfortably used. The monitor should be at a suitable distance and angle to avoid straining the neck. The image on the screen should be sharp and clear in a suitable colour scheme which will not be tiring on the eyes. The furniture should also be designed with these factors in mind – chairs which provide adequate back support and which allow the height and inclination of the seat to be adjusted should ideally be provided.

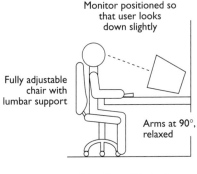

Monitor positioned so that user looks down slightly

Fully adjustable chair with lumbar support

Arms at 90°, relaxed

A healthy working position

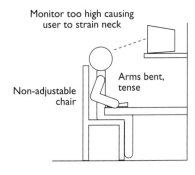

Monitor too high causing user to strain neck

Arms bent, tense

Non-adjustable chair

A poor working position

Windows pose problems in two ways. Having a window behind a screen will give a high contrast in lighting levels between the two that will be very difficult to work with. This should be avoided if possible, or at least some form of blind should be used on the window at the brighter times of the day/year. Secondly, windows (and other light sources) can give reflections on the screen. If these are a problem and cannot be resolved by moving either the screen or the light source, then consider using an anti-glare filter.

If you are using a computer for extended periods (eg all day at work), you should make a point of having frequent, regular short breaks away from the machine (even if just to do some other part of your job).

Good ventilation is also important to help create a comfortable working environment.

Index